Confronting Evil

Copyright © 2005 Richard A. Nable
All rights reserved.
ISBN: 1-4196-0263-2

To order additional copies, please contact us.
BookSurge, LLC
www.booksurge.com
1-866-308-6235
orders@booksurge.com

Big, Bald, Beautiful Man Productions,
In association with Gudluktuya Publications,
Presents:

Confronting Evil

Richard A. Nable

(Due to mature subject matter, reader discretion is advised.)

visit www.searchingforevil.com

2005

Confronting Evil

...there is no authority except from God, and those [authorities] which exist are established by God. Therefore he who resists authority has opposed the ordinance of God; and they who have opposed [authority] will receive condemnation upon themselves. ...if you do what is evil, be afraid: for [authority] does not bear the sword for nothing; for it is a minister of God, an avenger who brings wrath on the one who practices evil.... Render to all what is due them: ...fear to whom fear, honor to whom honor.

-Romans 13: 1-7

With power comes responsibility. Use it wisely.

CONTENTS

Introduction	XIII
Chapter One: What Makes a Sheepdog?	1
Chapter Two: Not Everyone Can Be A Sheepdog…	33
Chapter Three: Your Own Private Idaho	41
Chapter Four: Nable's Four P's of Reaction Dynamics	49
Chapter Five: Dah, Which Way Did He Go George?	61
Chapter Six: The Big Red Hump	85
Chapter Seven: The Best Laid Plans…	99
Chapter Eight: Here We Go Again	105
Chapter Nine: The Evil Drug Fairy	117
Chapter Ten: Why Do You think They Call It Dope?	127
Chapter Eleven: Super Evil	151
Chapter Twelve: Splattus Maximus	159
Chapter Thirteen: Let The Games Begin	173
Chapter Fourteen: Flim-Flams, Cons, and Scams	185
Chapter Fifteen: Baron Von Munchausen	195
Chapter Sixteen: A Garbage Slide You Say?	201
Chapter Seventeen: You're in the Army Now…	213
About The Author	229

INTRODUCTION

Sheepdog: (n) An individual who is part of that three to five percent of the world's population that is both environmentally and biologically predisposed to effectively confront the predators in society.

Richard Nable is a Sheepdog. Rich, as he is known to his friends, would not claim the title for his himself, nor would I claim it for myself. A person becomes a protector of society through a series of experiences and choices. This is called 'learning'. Experience teaches us which bits of knowledge that we possess really work. I was taught that there are two ways to learn; one is through experience, the other is through the experience of others. The problem with learning through experience is that you get the test before you get the lesson, and sometimes the lesson kills you. This book, "Confronting Evil", is a much less life threatening way to gain the experience that has shaped Rich (and some of his fellow officers as well) into a Sheepdog.

This is not a textbook in the strictest sense, although it does possess some of the elements of one. If you choose to read it as one you will not be disappointed. If, however, you choose to read it because you want to learn what it's like to be a Sheepdog or perhaps determine if you too are a sheepdog, you will be entertained and well rewarded for your effort.

Rich brings to the table in "Confronting Evil" a continuation of his somewhat whimsical look at the world we Cops live in. Insightful, knowledgeable, entertaining, and humorous are all words which describe this continuing journey into the world of law enforcement.

I have been in law enforcement for more than thirty years and a defender of society for more than fifty, since I took the Scout oath. I have known Rich Nable since he came to our agency. I could wax eloquent about his distinguished career and his many accomplishments. I could quote Heraclitus, but instead I'll quote Emery, "Even Heroes have Heroes." Rich is one of my Heroes.

Capt. P. R. Taylor
Retired

CHAPTER ONE
What Makes A Sheepdog?

Anyone who has ever owned a Sheepdog will tell you what incredibly loyal and loveable creatures they are. They are good-natured and have keen senses. They are strong and powerful yet usually very gentle. They are extremely intelligent and attractive animals as well.

When acting in a professional capacity, the Sheepdog is content to wander just outside, but always near his flock, constantly on guard. Often his only cohorts are the other Sheepdogs. Rarely do the sheep even notice he is there until that Evil wolf or a pack of Evil wild dogs come callin'. That's when the Sheepdog selflessly springs into action. His charming personality and friendly demeanor evaporate instantaneously. If the situation permits, he barks a stern and vicious warning. At times, his mere presence or his ominous growl is sufficient to set the would-be criminal straight, but other times Evil pays him no heed. Those are the times when that good-natured creature exercises his unique ability to instantly transform into an awesome and powerful beast who fearlessly confronts the predators who seek to harm his beloved flock. He will fight the intruders to the death if necessary because not only is that his job, it is his nature.

When the battle is won, the Sheepdog returns to his station. At times he will have to lick his wounds alone. At times his friends and family are by his side. He rarely has any reward other than the knowledge of a job well done, any comfort other than knowing that at least for the time being, the world is indeed a better place because of him. He knows that no matter how many wolves he deals with today, tomorrow there will be more. That knowledge does not discourage him, it empowers him. What is truly miraculous about the Sheepdog is that somehow he is able, time and time again, to transform himself from that awesome and powerful beast into that kind and gentle creature that we all love so much, because that too is his nature. He is a rare, magnificent and noble being.

When you work the streets long enough, you see all kinds of officers come and go. You learn to read them just like you do most everyone else in the world—all those walking, talking, dime-store novels. One common characteristic of the Sheepdog in training is that he or she always asks questions. There's no room for an ego when you're learning how to combat Evil on the front lines. Learning is part of the game. Those who are smart enough to realize that some of the older officers have a wealth of life saving and Evil catching wisdom locked away in their slippery little grey matter vaults, are usually smart enough to try anything they can to get their hands on that valuable commodity.

There is one question that over the years seems to crop up quite frequently among the callow little Sheepdog pups. That question is, "What makes a real PO-lice?"

I am quite confident that there are as many differing answers to that age old question as there are Sheepdogs to ask. I am still not sure that I have a concrete answer other than, "You know one when you see one." After much thought however, I can say that when an individual reaches the status of a "Real PO-lice", there are a few things that seem to run universally through the bloodline.

CONFRONTING EVIL

At some point in the individual's relentless pursuit of Evil, that true, blue blood police officer will have had a few experiences that, like some ancient rite of passage, seem to christen that individual with the aura of a warrior and endow him or her with the indomitable spirit of the Sheepdog. They seem to happen in no particular order and come with no fanfare or celebration. They simply happen and often are not fully appreciated for a long time to come.

There are three basic elements that give birth to a full fledged Sheepdog. They prove, both to the world at large and to the Sheepdog himself, that he or she has the mettle necessary to keep the faith without flinching and to endeavor to fight for Good regardless of circumstance or consequence.

Before one can become a Sheepdog, he must(For those who would cry a chauvinistic foul, anytime I refer to the Sheepdog as simply 'he', it is a generic 'he' and the she is also implied. It a real pain in the rear to keep typing 'he or she' all the time. Plus, if I type he/she then someone would likely think I was talking about one of those transitional transsexuals.), while combating Evil, be forced to taste his own blood. That taste serves as a flagrant and poignant reminder that he is not invincible and that underneath it all, all humanity shares at least one thing in common. It also proves that the individual is willing and capable of making the sacrifices that are characteristic of anyone who may choose the arduous task of defending all that which is honorable.

Similarly, at some point in the development of the Sheepdog, Evil forces the individual to taste his own sweat. The taste of sweat reminds us that the road we have chosen is a difficult one—not for the faint hearted or weak minded. Fortitude is required both in mind and body. Yet without the accompanying commitment, any effort to become a Sheepdog is wasted. Anything worth having is worth working for. There are indeed things in this life that are worth fighting for and there are even a few things that are worth dying for.

To round out the equation, Evil will, at some point, force the Sheepdog to taste his own tears. Our tears remind us of our own humility; a necessary ingredient for any true warrior. They also remind us that despite our best efforts, we have weaknesses that are as much a part of us and as necessary as our strengths. They make us human. Without humility, it is difficult to understand mercy, and mercy is one of the prime ingredients of Justice.

As I was writing the previous pages, I started to remember something that was said by a veteran officer when I had first joined the police department. Then I realized just how similar our three criteria happened to be for what makes a "real police officer". Though he was a good cop, he was not an educated man and probably had only finished high school. I doubt that the Sheepdog metaphor had made the rounds at that point in time but the similarities I think are obvious.

He said that before you could be considered a "real police officer", you had to get your ass kicked, catch a burglar single handedly and total a police car.

Here's my interpretation of those criteria:

Having your ass handed to you by a bad guy (or being forced to taste your own blood) teaches you a valuable lesson about humility. It also teaches you that no matter how bad you may think you are, you are not invincible. You have limitations and there is no shame in that. You have to be aware of your personal strengths and weaknesses to be effective. Though we do not always have a choice in the matter, it is better to teach yourself what your limitations are in a controlled environment rather than having someone else teach them to you on the street.

Besides getting an ass whippin', almost every good police

officer I have ever known has at some point in his career captured a burglar single handedly. Burglars are a particularly slippery bunch. Even though burglary is one of the most common of the major crimes and it costs US citizens somewhere around $3.3 billion per year in property loss (yes that's billion with a B), the burglar is one of the most difficult perpetrators to catch. His crime is usually hidden from the public eye or it is perpetrated so quickly that the only way to catch him is to be there when it happens.

Consequently, the Sheepdog that catches the elusive burglar wolf is one that is either incredibly lucky or, more likely, has honed his police skills to razor sharpness. Anyone who works that hard has undoubtedly tasted his own sweat and has probably done so more than once.

Lastly, a true police officer is one who is familiar with his own limitations and the limitations of his equipment. The only way to know your limitations is to exceed them from time to time to firmly cement that boundary in your psyche. By totaling your police car, you hopefully learn at least one of those boundaries and in a small way must taste your own tears.

Anyone who has been policing for any length of time has seen the type of officer who never takes a chance—the officer who is always safe and never does anything dangerous. While I am not advocating that anyone should act unsafely on purpose, the very nature of our job is danger. You cannot be a true police officer, a Sheepdog, without taking a risk every now and then. If those risks don't kill us, they most assuredly make us stronger.

Whenever I have a class full of rookies in an academy class, I try to make sure that I pose some challenging questions to the recruits to make them think. I ask things like, "What would you do if you came up to a convenience store and saw that the attendant inside was being robbed at gunpoint? What would you do if you rolled up on an apartment building that was engulfed in flames? What would you do if you were the first one to a call and saw a woman or a child about to be raped or murdered?" Sadly, the answer I get most often is something like, "I would wait for backup."

That answer is a "safe" answer. It may be the result of having too many administrators and/or trainers that have never been "real police" and just weren't born Sheepdogs. That answer could be the result of all the safety and liability issues we seem to overemphasize in every aspect of training. That answer could be the result of a non-Sheepdog analysis of a particular situation. That answer could be a mixture of all these ingredients or could be something that I haven't thought of yet.

Regardless, when true Evil is afoot and there's nothing between it and the innocent, a real police officer takes that risk and does whatever he or she can to protect the innocent and stop the Evil. Sure it's dangerous!!! It's the job we have chosen to do. While sometimes waiting for backup is a good idea, other times we may not be able to afford that luxury. To be a Sheepdog you must be willing to risk personal injury or even death, if the circumstance requires, in the fight against Evil. That is what makes a hero. That is what defines the Sheepdog.

There is no hierarchy to any of the Sheepdog elements I have discussed and I do not mean to suggest that they are exclusive to the Sheepdog. Nor do I dare suggest that these are the only ingredients in the Sheepdog mixture. They are merely things that observation has shown me seem to be a common thread among all those honorable men and women with whom I have had the privilege to serve. They are the 3-5% of the world's population that are destined to be Sheepdogs. It's not what they do, it's what they are. They really don't have a choice.

Somewhere around 500 BC, the philosopher/tactician

Heraclitus wrote, "For every one hundred men you send us, ten should not even be here. Eighty are nothing but targets. Nine of them are real fighters; we are lucky to have them, they the battle make. Ah, but the one. One of them is a warrior and he will bring the others back." Back then it was one percent Sheepdog. Now it's three to five percent. I will refrain from commenting on the statistical deviation but will simply point out that the theory is not new.

Now, to avoid some confusion between terms that I may seem to be using interchangeably, I want to make it clear that a "real police officer" or "real PO-lice" are always Sheepdogs but Sheepdogs are not always police officers. The broader category of Sheepdog includes people from virtually every walk of life that have some or all of the characteristics discussed here.

I remember an incident that happened outside of one of our large national-chain grocery stores. The call came in as a fight in progress but when I got there, as is often the case, the fight was over. There was a car in the middle of the congested parking lot that was haphazardly placed and still had its engine running but no one inside. There was a guy lying (not laying—please learn the difference) near the car. He was bloodied about the head and torso and looked unconscious. There was an old lady sitting down in a car with the door open who looked a little rattled and there was an average sized man in his thirties who looked a little upset and worried.

The last individual, the worried guy, was the one who approached me first when I arrived at the scene. He was very humble and apologetic and even started to get into the back of my patrol car. He was saying something like, "I didn't mean to really hurt the guy and if you need to arrest me I understand."

"Whoa, wait a minute. I need to find out what happened before I start deciding who goes to jail and who doesn't."

Some witness piped up saying, "That dude right there just

beat the crap out of that guy," as he motioned first toward the man who had spoken to me and then toward the man who was by then receiving medical attention from the paramedics.

A few other witnesses said basically the same thing. The next obvious direction for the investigation was to ask the alleged bad guy, "Why?"

The alleged bad guy then spoke a little more clearly and the whole thing started to make sense.

"I was here shopping with my mom. Because of her age she can't do a lot of stuff by herself. I was inside paying for the groceries and she started pushing the cart out to the car. When I came out of the store I saw that guy over there come runnin' up and knock her down and then he tried to steal her purse. I just reacted and came up and beat him. He was hurtin' my mama. She's an old lady. What king of guy does that? Anyway, that's what happened and I understand if you need to arrest me."

"Arrest you? Hell, I'd rather just shake your hand and give you a medal!"

After verifying that the man's story was a true and accurate account of what had transpired, I arrested the unconscious guy and told the other fellow that he was perfectly in the right and I would have done the exact same thing if I was in his position. It turns out that the car that was left running in the parking lot was the escape module for the old-woman-beatin', purse-snatchin' Evil. It also happened to be a stolen car. The man's mom was shaken but she didn't get hurt too badly considering what she had gone through. I also congratulated her for raising such a good son. Whether he knew it or not, I think he was part Sheepdog.

***

There is an old saying that goes, "The only reason that some people are alive is because no one has tried to kill them."

That could not be more true than it was for two officers who, fortunately for all of us, are no longer employed in a law enforcement capacity. Being a "Monday Morning Quarterback" has its obvious advantages yet also tends to draw the ire of individuals who say, "You have no right to criticize because you weren't there."

My response is, "That's what's so great about assuming the role of a Monday morning quarterback; you are unencumbered by all of those things that make decision making so difficult in the field." In our line of work, mistakes get people killed. I do have the right to criticize (as do we all) because that's how we learn. I encourage people all the time to criticize me and everyone else in our profession so that we can learn from our mistakes and see how other people would respond in the same situation. When you have the time to think through a problem you are much more capable of formulating an appropriate response than when you are under the pressure of the stressful moment. When you practice this problem solving technique regularly, you start to fill your mental toolbox with all kinds of things that you never would have gotten otherwise. That's one way a Sheepdog gets the edge.

The purpose behind Monday-morning-quarterbacking is not to criticize per se; it is to learn from other people's experiences and mistakes. Criticism is just a natural side effect of looking for ways to do something better than the guy before you. I know that having someone point out the things that you do right is good for stroking your ego but sometimes there's just not time for that. Hopefully, if and when you become an adult, your ego doesn't need quite so much stroking as it did when you were two! Therefore, if the person Monday-morning-quarterbacking you doesn't point out something as a mistake, then that means by default that you did that particular thing right. So if you need a pat on the back, do it yourself. Don't whine about not getting the pat from someone else.

I am about to Monday morning quarterback two officers in particular and if you think I am being too critical, you can stop reading. I keep myself and others alive by identifying screw-ups and trying to train people not to commit them. Criticism is not my primary intent but it is an unfortunate side effect of identifying errors.

Some readers may at first wonder why I chose to include this story in this particular chapter. The reason is simple: Sometimes a good way to illustrate a positive is to use a negative. I can give you a better idea of where North is if I show you South to go along with it.

At approximately 0130 hours one winter morning in the mid 1990s, a call came in to our dispatch center on an armed robbery. This was no ordinary armed robbery. Evil had the unmitigated gall (is there any other time that you can use the word unmitigated than preceding the word gall?) to perpetrate his despicable act at one of the most holy of law enforcement locales; the Donut Shop!

Two employees were in the store at the time when a scruffy looking African-American male, roughly forty years old, dressed entirely in black (Evil's hallmark fashion preference) entered the store and sat down at the counter near the door. He ordered four donuts and engaged the employees in some small talk, asking if the donut shop was hiring.

When he decided that the time was right, with a certain calm like the eye of a hurricane, he produced a black semi-auto pistol and pointed it at the employees.

"This is a stick-up. Stay calm and I won't kill you."

As easily as most people order hot coffee to go, he walked

around the counter and pressed his pistol into the ribs of one of the innocent employees.

"Open the register," he demanded.

The terrified clerk complied.

"Get over there," he barked, as he waved the pistol in the direction of the back room.

The employees did as they were told.

Evil then took all the paper money out of the register and put it in his pocket. Then he grabbed a to-go bag to put all the change in. Next he ripped the receiver out of the phone and gave one last order to the trembling donut shop attendants.

"Be calm. Wait 30 minutes before you call the police... I'll be back to rob ya'll again real soon."

Evil walked out of the donut shop and stopped long enough to speak to a woman who was sitting in her car in the parking lot just outside. He had no way of knowing that she was the mother of one of the employees he had just terrorized.

"The donut shop will be closed for the next 30 minutes," he said with a coolness that matched the still night air.

He left the scene on foot and disappeared into his natural environment.

Little did Evil know that the police were already on the way to the scene of the crime. The store manager had arrived at the store just in time to see Evil pointing his pistol at the cashier and had gone across the street to call 911.

As is so often the case, most of the officers were handling other calls and only one unit was in service and available. A second unit heard the call come out and vacated the call that he was on to start as a backup unit.

The first officer arrived at the scene and spoke briefly to the lady in the parking lot. That officer got a preliminary description and a direction of travel on the suspect and did what most good officers would do automatically; she went searching for Evil.

She turned down a nearby side street and casually scanned the area for someone matching the description of Evil. Apparently she was not expecting to find anything because Evil walked right up to her patrol car and pointed his gun in her face.

"Get out of the car!" he demanded.

The officer complied and later stated that she felt since he had the advantage she had no choice but to do what he said.

"Gimme your gun."

As sheepishly as she complied with the first request she granted Evil his second wish. It was around that time that she reached down and pressed the little orange button on the top of her radio that sent out an emergency tone to the dispatch center.

True to form and policy, the dispatcher immediately tried to raise the officer on the radio to find out what her emergency was. When there was no response, the radio operator activated the attention tone that broadcasts the equivalent of that annoying "Emergency Broadcast System" attention tone over all of the county radios.

Evil heard the attention tone and naturally demanded the officer's radio. As you might expect, the third wish was also granted.

"Walk towards those buildings," he said as he pressed the officer's own gun into her back.

"Have you got any money?"

"No," the officer said as they walked toward the rear of the building.

"Do you know me?"

"No."

"Good. You don't know me and I don't know you."

CONFRONTING EVIL

When they made it around to the back of the building, Evil had apparently not decided what he wanted to do.

"Lay on the ground. Face down. Put your hands on your head."

The officer had no problem assuming the customary execution position, yielding everything she had and everything she could ever hope to have to that pathetic excuse for a human being.

Something made Evil change his mind.

"Get up. We're goin' for a ride," he told the officer.

Once again, with all the substance and fortitude of an overboiled spaghetti noodle, the officer blindly did as ordered. As they walked back toward the officer's car, Evil also demanded that the officer hand over her extra magazines for the pistol he had already stolen. Once again she complied. They continued toward the police car.

Evil said, "I'll drive," and he headed for the driver's side of the patrol car.

Meanwhile, the second officer was looking for the first officer since no one had heard from her since she had activated her emergency tone. In a stroke of pure cop genius, the second officer drove up right behind the first officer's car as she was walking toward him in the company of Evil.

The second officer then declared over the radio that the first officer was OK without taking so much as a second to realize what was actually going on right in front of his dim little eyes.

Evil, feeling in complete control and empowered by the abject cowardice of the first officer, ran up to the second officer and did a repeat performance of his first hostage-taking exercise.

"Get out of the car or I'll shoot you."

The officer later said in his official statement, "Due to the nature of the situation I complied with his commands and exited my patrol vehicle. When I got out he still had me at gunpoint requesting that I give him my weapon. I asked the subject not to shoot in which he replied, I'm not going to shoot you. You're a brother."

Evil took the officer's gun out of the holster without so much as a protest.

During this time, the first officer was being completely ignored by Evil, so what did she do?

She could have pulled out her extra gun and ended the situation in the abrupt and violent manner that would have been so appropriate but she wasn't the type of officer to be burdened with something like carrying an extra weapon.

She could have obeyed the first rule of armed combat which states: Exit the kill zone.

She didn't do that either.

Instead, she chose to "low crawl" back to her police car to get to that all important radio to call for a Sheepdog to come and rescue her. Even that effort was botched since in her emotional state she called out on the wrong radio channel so it took a while for anyone to realize what was going on.

Meanwhile, Evil directed the second officer to get into the first patrol car with the other officer. The second officer had no back-up weapon either.

Evil then left the scene in the second officer's patrol car. The first two officers "attempted to follow" Evil in the remaining patrol car but of course lost sight of Evil almost immediately.

To add one last insult to injury, the last line of the second officer's statement reads, "My bullet proof vest was in my patrol vehicle at the time of the theft."

I couldn't make up a story like that if I had to because I would never think that something like that could happen in real life. Every detail is accurate and complete and together they offer a plethora of lessons to be learned. Rarely does making one mistake cause an officer too much trouble. Most officers who find themselves in a "world of shit" end up there as the result of a chain of mistakes.

It certainly seems to me that both of these officers had one thing in common: they never really considered the possibility that they might come face to face with Evil. Whether it is the fact that at least one of the officers left his protective vest in his police car or that neither officer approached either scene with any regard for basic tactical procedures, these officers are the epitome of the mindset that gets people killed.

The first time that Evil approached either officer, the officer was in a police car. My first thought would be to drive away. When you are so utterly taken by surprise and have not previously formulated an escape plan, you are likely to freeze. That is precisely what happened here.

Let's not forget that each officer knew that they were looking for an armed robber yet neither had prepared for that meeting. Their alertness level should have been heightened to the point where no one could possibly sneak up on them, yet it happened not once but twice.

In my nearly two decades of working the street, never once has anyone approached my police car without my knowledge. My standard practice, if I cannot get out of my car to meet someone who is approaching me, is to draw my weapon and hold it close to my torso in a hidden "cover" position. Any sign of a threat means that Evil takes a minimum of one round point blank and probably many more. I can hear the liberal pansies screaming, "You can't just point guns at people…" blah blah blah.

I really don't care if someone gets offended as long as I get to leave the encounter alive. Incidentally, none of the literally dozens of people that I have pointed my pistol at in the aforementioned manner ever even saw the gun that was only inches from them. Like the officers in the story, they don't expect to see a gun in my hand so they don't unless I do something to draw attention to it (which I don't).

I think that anyone with even a smidgeon of tactical sense can identify any number of times after the first officer met Evil, that a moderately skilled fighter or mediocre marksman could have put an end to the confrontation. The first such situation that comes to mind is when Evil asked the officer to hand over her firearm. My advice is never give up your primary weapon until you have dispensed all of the ammunition, preferably into the body and/or head of a well deserving Evil—and what better time to do so than when Evil asks for it?

Never assume, as the second officer did, that because an officer (or anyone else) is walking with a stranger that everything is okay. Take a moment to consciously assess a situation before you make a decision on what you are seeing. Later in the book you will see this referred to as the processing phase. Proper processing is a key ingredient in the proper handling of an incident.

Always have a plan B. I can never say that enough times or with enough emphasis. A natural segue from the topic of plan B is to always leave yourself an escape route so, if something does take you by surprise, you can make a tactical withdrawal to regroup and attack or, at the bare minimum, you can dodge whatever gets thrown at you. There is no victory in defense.

Perhaps one thing we try to hammer into recruits is that no matter what happens you never give up. You fight tooth and nail with every bit of life and breath and strength that you have because in real life there are no do-overs. These two officers seemed to give up before the fight ever even began.

Some pacifist sissy whiners will undoubtedly point to the fact that since neither officer was killed, then their actions were appropriate. To that I retort with an emphatic, "Bullshit!" Those officers had no idea how that situation was going to turn out, yet they laid their own lives in the hands of Evil and rolled the dice without so much as a whimper of resistance. We can all infer from Evil's statement that had the second officer been of any race other than Evil's, he would have been dead right there.

There is no place in police work for the frame of mind those two officers had. Not everyone is cut out for police work. On the contrary, very few people are ideally suited for it. I am thankful that both officers realized that they had made a mistake in their chosen careers and decided to move on. I bear them no bad feelings. It is not their fault that they are the way that they are. There are plenty of other ways that they can make their contribution to Society.

As a rule, the determination of whether or not someone is a Sheepdog is a right reserved to that person's peers. That is one reason why none of the stories in this chapter are about me. If I am to be granted the exalted high honor of Sheepdog, it is not my place to say. I can, however, bestow that honor on those kindred spirits with whom I serve.

My last entry for this chapter not only has a much happier ending, it has my brother as its main character. He is also a police officer and he works for the same department I do. When I started policing, he was stuck in some dull and boring, computer related job that probably made a moderately good use of his degree in mathematics but did little to stimulate the Sheepdog within. He lived on my beat at the time and I would sometimes visit him while on duty and tell him some of my "war stories." I think he just got tired of hearing about all the fun I was having at work and salary be damned, he went and signed up. Though he is three years older, he is still a year behind me in police work which means to me he will always be a rookie!

The story you are about to read is told primarily in his own words with only a few things edited to fit my format. The story is informative, entertaining, compelling and maybe even emotional, but most importantly, like everything else in this book, it is all true.

02/08/96: It was a night like any other in February. A little warm for

the season but not hot by any means. Officer Barclay Brinson and I were headed east on Old Alabama Road (in separate cars) in an effort to try to get a Wendy's hamburger before the next call. I was on the DUI Task Force but had been assigned to help out the patrol division on the evening watch until some people got out of training and filled the gaps left by the recent exodus of officers to more lucrative jobs elsewhere.

We had just turned north on Medlock Bridge Road (GA hwy 141)

when officer Brinson got a radio call.

"330", the radio operator said.

"330, go ahead", officer Brinson properly responded.

"330, Signal 24 violent at 2725 Greenhouse Parkway."

"330 received."

Officer Brinson made a U-Turn at a break in the concrete median and I did the same, knowing that the nearest backup unit was all the way on the other side of the county.

"373," came the radio call.

"373," I responded knowing that the dispatcher was going to send me with Brinson as backup.

"373, start with 330 to the Signal 24."

"373, I'm already enroute."

I had only known officer Brinson for a short time because he was fresh out of Field Training. I bet he probably hadn't been on the street by himself for more than 5 or 6 months. But, I also knew that he was one of the better officers we had on our department, despite his lack of experience. I would much rather have been on a call with him than lots of other officers in the department who had been around a lot longer.

I looked down at the KDT (a mobile computer terminal mounted in my patrol car) and read the text that had been sent to me by the dispatcher. The signal was 24, a demented person, and the text that had been entered by the call taker in the communications center told me that the person had a history of suicide attempts and that the call had come from a mental health facility. I also saw that the person's last name from the E911 information was DIBONA. I wondered to myself if she was any relation to Vin DiBona of television fame. Bob Sagett is always making jokes about Mr. DiBona on the show America's Funniest Home Videos. I dismissed that as a silly idea and continued to follow officer Brinson westbound on Old Alabama Road.

We were fairly far from Greenhouse Patio Apartments so we decided, via KDT messages, that after we cleared the call we would get our burger at the McDonald's on Holcomb Bridge Road at Nesbit Ferry Road rather than drive all the way back up to Wendy's. The Wendy's was just across the Forsyth County line at the intersection of Medlock Bridge Road and McGinnis Ferry Road. Besides, we were the only two cars on the entire east side of GA Hwy 400 and most of the calls for police service were in the area of Holcomb Bridge Road, so it made more sense for us to try to stay around that area.

We arrived at the intersection of Nesbit Ferry Road and Holcomb Bridge Road a few minutes later and stopped for the red light. When the light turned green, officer Brinson's rookieness became apparent, but only in a minor way. He turned left on Holcomb Bridge to go to the main entrance of Greenhouse Patio Apts. I went straight, knowing from seven and one-half years of experience that the rear entrance would put me closer to building number 27.

I saw a sign indicating that buildings 25-27 were down the first drive to the left after crossing Holcomb Bridge Road. I was rewarded with the vain satisfaction that my vast experience and familiarity with the area that would make a cartographer proud had given me a response time of a full 60 seconds shorter than that of officer Brinson. Whoopie! I drove past building 25 and followed the drive around to the right and located building 27.

I am always irritated when I arrive at an apartment complex and the buildings are poorly labeled. Even when I am fortunate enough to locate the right building, there are usually several breezeways and it sometimes takes two or three attempts to locate the correct apartment.

This complex, fortunately, had not only put large numbers on the side of each building, but had also labeled each entrance with the apartment numbers that could be accessed from each particular breezeway. With my right side alley light I was able to read the sign and see that the apartment I was looking for was on the north end of building 27. I double-parked behind some vehicles in front of building 27 and left my parking lights on.

From the point of view of a police officer, double parking like that can serve several purposes, the main one being safety. As long as there is no tactical reason to be completely hidden from view, this method of parking is desirable. If an officer has to call for help, it is easier for the responding officer to look for a set of parking lights in the middle of a drive rather than stop to try to read the numbers on each building. If the patrol car is parked in a space with lights out like all the other vehicles, it blends in and it makes it hard for help to locate you, something that could be very important if the proverbial shit hits the fan. I have tried to instill this practice in new officers that I come into contact with just as I did that night with officer Brinson.

Double parking may also block a vehicle that may try to flee the scene of a crime in case the perpetrator tries to make an escape. Lastly, it is a lot easier to park that way and it reduces the chance that the officer will damage a patrol car or citizen's car trying to park and/or back up. I know that the Chief would love to have fewer damaged county cars.

In the spirit of good fun, I decided that I would show officer Brinson that I had a sense of humor. I got out of my car and leaned up against the trunk. I took a posture of relaxation with my arms crossed as if to say, "what took so long?"

When Brinson finally pulled in behind me, I noticed that he left his headlights on because his Ford Crown Victoria is equipped with headlights that turn off automatically. It's a nice option but one that has no practical use in police-work. I began to explain to him the purpose in leaving parking lights on.

Brinson agreed with my point and we began to walk toward the breezeway of building 27. We followed a narrow concrete walkway about 30 feet into the north breezeway of building 27.

"What apartment number are we looking for again?"

"2725," Brinson responded.

"That's what I thought." I said at the same time that I noticed the numbers on the door to my right had a 1 as the third digit. This was obviously a complex that had chosen to use the building number as the first two digits of the apartment number, the floor number as the third digit and the unit number as the fourth digit. That meant that apartment 2725 would be one floor above us.

We were walking side by side. Brinson was on my right.

He is about 5 feet seven or eight inches tall, has an average build and wears a Marine style high and tight haircut (probably because he is in the Marine Corps Reserve). As we were walking and talking the mood was business as usual, but that quickly changed when we heard some sort of commotion in an apartment above us.

"I bet that would be it," Brinson said as we both looked up in the direction of the noise.

It was a woman's voice that we had heard. The voice was clearly agitated but we could not make out the words. Nor could we tell if the woman was screaming for help or was simply involved in an argument.

Brinson ascended the concrete steps to the first landing and then turned to ascend the final set of steps to the top. As I followed along several steps behind, I looked up through the railing balusters to see what we were getting into. I noticed that the six-panel, metal door to apartment 2725 was not completely closed. The door was resting on the inner edge of the door jamb.

"Door's not closed." I told Brinson as he took a position at the top of the stairs next to the door to apartment 2725.

Brinson didn't respond, but I knew he heard me.

As I came up the steps behind him, I saw that Brinson had unholstered his sidearm, a Berretta Model 92F 9mm handgun, and was holding it down by his right thigh. I was glad to see that this rookie was more concerned about safety than appearance. I believe it is better to have and not need than to need and not have, certainly when things could get violent. Also, I'd rather answer to a citizen complaint about me or another officer drawing his or her weapon than not to have that weapon ready when needed.

Since Brinson had his handgun out and we could still hear some commotion in the apartment, I did not un-holster my pistol. Instead, I used my left hand (non-weapon hand) to remove my pepper spray canister from its holder. I checked to see that my grip was correct. I didn't want to spray it in my own face if it became necessary to use it.

"POLICE," Brinson said in a firm voice as he knocked on the door with his left hand.

His call was answered by an unseen person on the inside of the apartment abruptly slamming the door to its fully closed position. It was obvious that there was some sort of fight going on inside at this point, so I moved past Brinson and took a position on the opposite side of the door. As I did so I noticed that there was a duffle bag sitting outside the door on the left. It was not closed and it appeared that it was filled with clothing and other personal belongings. The thought occurred to me that this may be a domestic situation and one of the parties was intending to leave or maybe one of the parties was trying to force the other to leave. I filed that away in the back of my head and concentrated on the present.

I was holding the pepper spray behind me on the left to maintain the element of surprise. If I had to spray someone I would rather it be a surprise to them. I pulled it into view for just a second so that Brinson could see that I had that avenue covered. I didn't want him to be surprised if it became necessary to spray someone.

When officers work together on a regular basis, a relationship develops that is difficult to explain. Many times in the past I have gone to calls with officers who are close friends of mine and we know each other and each other's habits and methods so well that we rarely need to talk over a plan of action. It just comes naturally when working with close friends or partners.

However, I had never been on a call with Brinson and I only knew him from a minimal amount of casual hellos as we crossed paths at the precinct or in similar chance encounters.

"Police!" Brinson called out as he knocked firmly on the apartment door again.

I leaned down, putting my left ear as close to the door as possible to try to hear what the commotion was. At the same time I noticed that Brinson reached out with his left hand and shook the door knob, testing to see if the knob was locked. It was.

"What is she saying?" I thought to myself. The sounds seemed not quite as close to the door as I had expected. Maybe the woman had moved to a back room.

My mind began to consider different courses of action.

"Is she crying out for help? Should I kick the door, call for another car, what?" I thought.

I just couldn't hear her words clearly and I didn't hear any signs of a struggle. No one had told me, but somehow I came to the conclusion that there must be another person inside, but what was happening?

All of that didn't matter because just as I stepped back from the door, I looked at Brinson and was about to speak. He looked at me and seemed he was also about to say something when suddenly the door flew open and a woman came running out.

She stepped off to my one o'clock position and leaned on the railing next to the apartment door that was directly across from her own. She was clearly agitated. She was shaking and had her head in her hands as she spoke.

"Help me!" She screamed. "He's inside and he's got a knife!" She cried as the door she ran out of slammed shut behind her.

Suddenly, this routine 24 call had taken a turn for the worse, and later would take a turn for the worst. A man with a knife is nothing to take lightly. In training we had been taught the 21 foot rule. A man with a knife who is closer than 21 feet can charge and stab you before you have a chance to draw your weapon and defend yourself if you are caught unaware. 21 feet seems like a long way but I was about to find out how short a distance that really is.

Knowing that a knife can be a very deadly weapon, I drew my gun. Years of mental and physical practice had made me just as comfortable holding a gun as I am driving a car or any other daily activity. I don't remember how the gun felt in my hand because my attention was fixed on the door of the apartment.

With pepper spray in my left hand and my service weapon in my right, I stood at the ready, not knowing what was waiting on the other side of that door.

My position was a poor one. I was on the hinge side of the door and the door opened away from me which meant that I had no cover or concealment from a person opening the door from the inside. Brinson was on the knob side so he had at least a little concealment from the wall that was beside him.

"Okay, let's not rush into anything," I thought. Many times officers have been hurt when they rushed into a situation that they knew nothing about. There is some sort of mental tough guy attitude that sometimes takes over, a desire to be the one in control, the hero, the parent, so to speak.

One thing my experience had taught me was that by the grace of God I had not been hurt all those times in the past when I had rushed into a situation I knew nothing about. Many times I have reflected on past incidents and realized that if someone had been so inclined, the opportunity to hurt or kill me was there. Thank you, Lord, for being my protector.

Three loud, forceful knocks on the door marked the third and final time we would identify ourselves as police officers. In the blink of an eye the door flew open to reveal a man. He was a white male, tall and slim like me, holding not one but two knives. In his right hand was a large kitchen knife. The silver blade was eight, maybe nine inches in length. The base of the blade was the same width as the white handle. The blade was straight on the blunt side and curved as it widened toward the end on the sharp side.

In his left hand he clutched an inexpensive looking steak knife with a blade that was serrated from the tip to the hilt. He held that knife close to his body near the left side of his gut. Strangely, he had wrapped the handle in a piece of white cloth.

My first though was disbelief. This guy was not going to quit attacking this woman even though the police were there. It is amazing how fast the human mind can ponder things. In that instant I thought of the FATS (FireArms Training Simulator) machine and a similar shoot/don't shoot simulation I had trained with before.

The FATS machine is a great training device. I have an opportunity to train on the FATS machine every time I am required to qualify at the firing range with my issued weapon.

In a FATS simulation, the officer is in a room facing a large movie screen. Behind the officer is the operator. A projection TV box is on the floor about eight feet from the screen and a device resembling a tripod mounted video camera is positioned to the left of the screen. The room is darkened and the officer is instructed to load his weapon with special plastic caps. They look like ammunition casings with a small primer in them and nothing else. The operator loads a scenario into the computer and the officer waits for the simulation to begin.

The officer is expected to use good judgment, verbal commands, and cover when available. Most of all, the officer is expected to decide whether or not deadly force is justified. The FATS machine presents the officer with a scenario and if the officer chooses to shoot, the machine stops the scenario when a lethal hit is detected. If the officer chooses not to shoot, the scenario ends when the incident is over. The officer must then explain to the operator why he took the action he did and the operator critiques the officer's performance. What a great tool!

Anyway, back to the story. Suddenly my mind realized what the real intention of this man was. He was coming at me! I suppose I got tunnel vision when I saw that he was coming at me because I don't remember seeing anything but the man charging at me with the knives. Even though he was a fairly tall man, his posture was not good. He stood slightly bent over as he came at me. He never said a word and he never looked me in the face. He had a glazed look, almost as if he was in world all his own.

He stared straight at my torso as he ran at me and it seemed as though he was looking right through me. As he got closer I saw that his right arm was extending out toward me and I began to move backwards. In a flash he was on me and as I backed up I looked down and saw the tip of the knife touch me on the flap of my right side breast pocket. Even though I was wearing a bulletproof vest, I felt pressure on my chest.

That was all I felt because at that same instant I dropped my pepper spray and fired three times. The shots were nothing like what you see on television. No loud bang; just a quick pop, pop, pop. Then the man fell to the floor.

I didn't hear the sound of the empty brass casings when they came to rest ten feet below on the concrete breezeway, nor did I feel the impact when my right shoulder hit the post that extends from floor to ceiling, supporting the hand rail at the top of the flight of stairs that was behind me.

God's providence saw to it that the post kept me from falling backwards down the steps and to the ground below. I surely would have felt that.

Evil landed on his left side, the knife falling free of his right hand and coming to rest at the base of the wall. He was still alive but not for long. All three of my shots had found their mark and had mortally wounded the knife wielding man. As he rolled over into a prone position, I saw the steak knife still in his left hand near his stomach and then it disappeared under his body.

The smell of gunpowder hit my nose and then vanished, carried away by the flow of air through the breezeway. Evil let out a labored groan and tried to roll back to his side. I holstered my weapon after I had subconsciously thumbed the decocking lever down and then up again to put the weapon back in the double action mode. That is what I was trained to do. Blood was beginning to pour out of Evil's chest and was making a puddle on the concrete floor. With my left foot I touched him on his right hip and told him to stay down and that help was on the way.

Brinson screamed into the radio an unintelligible call for help while still covering the man with his pistol. I motioned to him with my left hand to stop and then I called for help. Rookies get a little excited sometimes and talk too loud and fast on the radio. I know I have been guilty of that offense several times. It's hard not to yell when you're in the middle of a bad situation and need help two minutes ago.

"373 to radio," I said in a clear but urgent tone. "Start me Rescue and a 4 (ambulance). I have signal 50d (shot) the perpetrator. He tried to 51 me!"

"Received 373," was the operator's only response.

"Oh my God!" screamed the woman. "You didn't have to shoot him. He just needed some help."

"Uuuuuuggggh." A muffled moan came from Evil as he rolled back onto his stomach. His glasses were pushed off his face by the concrete floor as his muscles became too weak to hold his head up. That was the last sound he made. Death, mercifully, came quickly for him and he gave up his ghost.

Evil's color rapidly turned to a pale ashen gray as I stepped over his body toward the woman.

"He gave me no choice," I said to the woman, holding back any anger I had toward her, knowing that she had every right to be upset at the situation. I didn't say any more to her about it, knowing that when she calmed down and pondered the situation, she would realize that I had no other course of action than the one I had taken.

Of course, all of this commotion brought the neighbors out of their apartments and every officer who heard the radio call came to offer whatever assistance was needed. The residents soon calmed themselves and went back inside their homes. Officers, detectives, supervisors and the news media all came and went as expected. I was put on administrative leave while the incident was investigated. During the following week I was sent to a psychologist to ensure I wasn't having any mental malfunctions as a result of the shooting. At the same time, the detectives concluded their investigation and determined, as I already knew, that the shooting was completely justified.

In the years since the shooting I have thought and talked about the incident several times and have come to some conclusions. I learned later that the man who had tried to stab me was suffering from mental problems. Apparently, when he took his medication he was a good and productive member of society. He was a chemist for a national cosmetics company and an aspiring artist. It was when he failed to take his medication that he became a danger to himself and others. Based on the things I have learned about him since the shooting, I have come to believe that he committed what's known as "Suicide by Cop"—a phenomenon wherein a person wishes to die but cannot commit suicide alone. He therefore engages in conduct toward a police officer which he knows will be responded to with deadly force. I believe it was his decision to die and he used me as the instrument of his death.

One interesting side effect this incident has had on me is in my dreams. Most officers report that they have dreams of life or death encounters that end unfavorably for the officer. Officers, me included, report dreaming of encountering gun wielding perpetrators and when the officer decides in his dream to shoot back, the bullets just fall out of the gun or hit the suspect with no effect. These dreams can be very frustrating for officers—they were for me. I say they 'were' because since this incident I have not had any more dreams like that. Perhaps my subconscious is now convinced that when life or death situations present themselves, I am capable of making good choices and ensuring a favorable outcome—favorable for me that is.

Some officers who have been involved in situations similar to this end up with psychological problems and some even develop PTSD (Post Traumatic Stress Disorder). I truly believe I have been spared those afflictions because of several very important factors. In the years before the incident, I pondered the possibility that I would be forced to shoot someone and prepared myself for it. I am a Christian and believe all human life is precious. I also believe that all humans have a God given right to protect themselves and others from those who would seek to put their lives or the lives of others in jeopardy. In the past, when I asked myself if I would be able to use deadly force against someone, I always answered yes. If you cannot answer yes to that question every time it is asked, then perhaps the role of police officer, Sheepdog, or gun owner for that matter, is not the one for you. God has equipped me well both physically and mentally for this life I have chosen. I have never wanted to kill another human being, but on that fateful day I had no other choice. God willing I'll not have to experience something like that again, but if I do, my faith, morals and ethics will give me all the strength I need.

Those directly affected by this incident may never be able to see what good can come out of such a tragedy, but I'll leave the reader with this final thought from Romans 8:28. "And we know that God causes all things to work together for good to those who love God, to those who are called according to His purpose."

※※※

Sheepdogs in training always seem to want to ask about "scenarios". They want to know about specific examples of how to handle certain situations. I usually give in to the request a time or two before I explain one simple rule that I have in teaching. Specific examples should only be used to teach general principles by showing how those principles can be applied. If you only learn specific applications, then the only thing you learn is how to handle specific situations. Those specific situations may never occur again; making the knowledge useless and the time spent learning it wasted.

I try to make sure that my students learn the general principles behind the specific applications so that they can learn how to apply those principles to any potential threat or situation that they may encounter. As the old Chinese proverb goes, "Give a man a fish; feed him for a day. Teach a man to fish; feed him for a lifetime." (The original saying is widely attributed to the philosopher Lao Tzu. Some more modern, alternate endings are: ...and he'll sit in a boat and drink beer all day, ...and he'll soon die from mercury poisoning, ...and you'll get rid of him for a whole weekend. While the last three are kind of funny, I prefer the original.)

I trust that the preceding anecdotes have adequately illustrated the concept of the Sheepdog. There are no limits of race or sex, religion, nationality, age, political preference, sexual orientation or any other similar caste or category placed on who is allowed to be a Sheepdog. You either are or you aren't; period.

As for Evil, sometimes it is the sum total of a person's life pursuits. Other times it is a single poor decision or a mental or psychological malfunction. As used in this book, the term Evil merely refers to an action in and of itself and is not meant as a commentary on any person's worth as a human being in general. People who are essentially Good, can in fact do things that are Evil. For some, Evil is all they know.

CHAPTER TWO

Not Everyone Can Be A Sheepdog… But This Is Ridiculous

I remember watching television as a teen and seeing a number of TV shows and even some news reports that showed residents in large US cities who would virtually ignore other citizens in trouble or crimes in progress. That mentality ran contrary to everything I had ever been taught and none of the people I knew behaved that way. That was just another glimpse of the "real" world that just did not make any sense to me. To be honest, I thought it was an exaggeration to say the least.

As with many other areas of life, when I became a police officer I also became enlightened to the way the world really is. I am thankful to say that at least where I am, the people are still not as apathetic as I remember the examples from TV in my teen years, but there have been a few instances that have really flabbergasted me. (Isn't flabbergasted a great word?)

In my opinion, being a good American or even just being a good person means wanting to help your fellow man and actually stepping up to the plate and following through when someone is in need. Maybe we all become a little numb to the needs of our fellow man when they don't seem to us to be quite so severe or when we perceive that our own needs are more important, but I think we would all agree that a life or death situation is something that might warrant the attention of a stranger. Even if all you do is call 911, at least you have done something. Not everyone is a Sheepdog. Not everyone is equipped to intervene in a crime in progress or save someone from the clutches of Evil because of whatever their own physical, emotional or mental limitations may be, but how hard is it to dial a phone...or even to ask someone else to dial it?

I was sitting in a parking lot watching one of our high crime venues, with a trainee in the car with me and another veteran officer in his own car parked next to me. Not much was going on but that didn't keep us from watching and hoping. Radio called my unit and directed me to start for a call on multiple shots fired about a block from our current location. Most gunshots are fairly loud and over the years you learn to listen for even the faint, far-off ones, but I hadn't heard a thing and neither had any of the officers with me. In this particular neighborhood, shots were not an uncommon occurrence.

What we did hear was the sound of one of those large trash trucks emptying a dumpster. For those of you who are not familiar, when those trucks pick up and dump a big steel dumpster, the slapping of the metal doors makes some pretty loud bangs. Often those bangs are called in as gunshots. Naturally, we assumed that those sounds were what the caller had heard.

Nevertheless, like good little officers, we checked the area rather than dismissing the call based on an assumption. After all, assumption is the mother of all screw ups. The only information we were given was that the shots were heard near "an intersection" so we proceeded to that intersection and, finding nothing, began to patrol through the several apartment complexes that bordered the intersection. In this particular case, we actually spent a bit more time hunting for the phantom shots than is normally the practice but we still came up empty.

While we were checking the area, another officer coming in behind us stopped a young man who was running down the road for no apparent reason. He did the routine check and came up with nothing, so he let the guy go. A few hours later, I was off work and working an extra-job directing traffic when a call came over the radio to start for a man down in a courtyard of one of the apartment complexes we had checked earlier that morning.

As the units slowly responded to the scene, I overheard one of them start a supervisor and a detective. Naturally my ears perked up and I listened further. Before my extra-job was over, I learned that they were working a homicide. Thinking that I may have inadvertently overlooked a dead guy, I wanted to be sure that they knew about our shots fired call and that we did actually look around the neighborhood. I also wanted to see the dead guy and where he was. I actually went to the crime scene when I was off duty (which for me is a little out of character) and spoke to the detectives.

Apparently, at around the time of our loud dumpster/shots fired call, a young man happened to be running for his life from someone who was obviously very angry with him. With what I would call stellar marksmanship, Evil had shot this guy about six times in the back while he was running away. The spontaneous bullet sponge promptly collapsed and died on the stairs next to the pool in a wide open courtyard which, I might add, was not visible from the parking lot and was a fair distance from that intersection to which we had been dispatched.

To add insult to fatal injury, after canvassing the area we learned that a number of residents had seen the body but did not think it was important enough to call the police. They apparently thought he was drunk or was suffering from some other, similar malady. Several residents had also heard the gunshots but didn't think that was important either. There were residents who even confessed to stepping over his body on the way to work, not realizing and more importantly not caring that he was dead.

It eventually turned out that the guy who was running down the road was a witness to the crime and he didn't want to get any more involved in the situation than he already was. The shooter was allegedly a gang-banger/drug dealer and the dead guy violated some rule of the Evil club for which he had to be summarily dismissed. Regardless of who or why, it still disturbs me that things like that happen within full knowledge of numerous individuals who do not feel compelled to contact anyone or do anything!

Now, if you think that was bad, wait until you get a load of this. I was on my way to the precinct to turn in some paperwork at about three or four o'clock in the morning. The night had been fairly slow and I really had nothing better to do. To be honest, I really didn't want anything to do. I was almost to the station (which is fairly far from my beat) when radio gave out a call on a fight in progress in the parking lot of an apartment complex. I was only about 100 yards away from the entrance to that very same complex, and about a half mile from the fight itself. Fight calls are fairly routine and normally I would have let the beat car handle it but dispatch added one little bit of information that made me think that this was no ordinary fight call. She said that two or three males were beating up another male in the parking lot in front of the caller's apartment. Something just didn't feel right.

By the time I was able to let the dispatcher know that I was close to the call and would be responding, I was already in the complex. That particular complex is fairly large and has only one way in and one way out. The entrance is a fairly long, divided parkway. I was trying to watch the cars exiting as I was entering to see if I could spot anyone suspicious. One or two cars passed and then a third, but they did not exhibit any behavior that sent up a red flag.

However, as I got to a small, four-way stop inside the complex, two cars approached from my left. They were very close to each other and just didn't look quite right. I watched them as they passed me and the occupants were stiff as boards. They didn't make one move to look at me and, for reasons that were both tangible and intangible, they were the definition of a red flag.

At that point, I had very little information to go on. No suspect description of any kind, no mention of any vehicles, and no real positive information on the fight other than what I have already mentioned. I had to decide either to attempt a traffic stop on these two cars or go onto the scene to find out what, if anything, had happened.

What I elected to do was to watch the cars pass, give a description of each and a tag number from the only one that I could read. I then continued to the location of the fight. I felt certain that one of the other dispatched units would be close behind and could stop the two cars before they made it out of the long driveway of the apartment complex. I could then go and ascertain if anything had happened and advise the other units accordingly.

As I made my way through the sprawling complex to the site of the alleged fight, I came upon a very eerie and surreal scene. The parking lot opened fairly wide as I was at the area where residents parked their boats, RVs and other large vehicles. The yellow-orange light of the sodium-vapor streetlamps cast a peculiar, haunting glow across the parking lot. I seem to remember a faint mist hovering close to the ground which only added to the effect. There was a dark colored SUV to my left and about fifty feet away. It was just sitting there with its headlights on as if someone had left it in a hurry. There was a fair amount of unidentifiable debris that was a mixture of dirt and trash and who knows what, scattered across the pavement. A little closer to me and to my right was the unmistakable form of a body.

As I walked closer to the body, I noticed that there were skid marks all around the area that looked fresh. The body was now definitely that of a man and most of his clothes were gone. I immediately started an ambulance and paramedics and went to check on his condition. As I got even closer I noticed that one set of those skid marks seemed to go right over the body. There were even tire tracks left on his skin.

I let radio know that those two cars I had seen were very likely involved and that they needed to be stopped. Little did I know that there were no other officers anywhere nearby. I looked over the victim briefly while a timid looking person with a cordless phone in his hand cautiously approached from the shadows of one of the buildings to my left. There were no external injuries on the victim and he was still breathing so there wasn't a whole lot that I could do for him. Let me clarify one thing here. The victim was breathing, but it was that heavy, irregular breathing that is so common in people who are severely injured. Almost everyone I have seen in that condition has died shortly thereafter.

I knew that the guy had been run over at least once and could only assume that he was near death. It took forever to get any help there and I felt bad because I literally could do nothing for the poor man. I took a minute to speak to the man who approached me with the phone and found out that he was a friend of the man on the ground. I asked what had happened and listened as he gave a disjointed and emotional account of a fight between the victim and three or four other guys.

I won't bore you with the details but eventually we were

able to discover that the man on the phone (witness) and the victim had been out drinking at a neighborhood bar earlier in the evening. Several other guys at the bar had made some inappropriate comments to the witness' sister and a verbal altercation broke out. The girls left and then so did the antagonizers, while the witness and the victim stayed for a few more minutes.

When they had cooled down, they too left and headed for home. Apparently Evil had been lurking in the shadows (as Evil often does) and followed the two men back to their apartment complex. As the witness and the victim were parking their car, one of the men approached with his hand under his shirt. He told the victim to "give up his muther fuckin money" and gestured with the concealed hand as if to imply the presence of a weapon.

The victim got offended rather than scared and got out of his truck reaching for the concealed hand of Evil number one. (I have no doubt in my mind that he ingested some liquid courage earlier in the evening which contributed to his behavior and ultimately to his demise.) When the victim grabbed Evil's hand, he realized that Evil only had a wine bottle. With that revelation the fight was on. Unfortunately, most criminals are cowards and this guy was no different. He probably would have gotten his ass whipped if his friends hadn't joined in. They proceeded to beat the victim down (four against one) in the parking lot until the victim was nearly unconscious. Then they turned to leave.

Our victim, not knowing when to quit, struggled to his feet and ran back to his truck to get a baseball bat. As Evil tried to drive off, the victim bashed in the side of Evil's SUV with the baseball bat. Evil got really pissed.

Evil began chasing the victim through the parking lot in the baseball bat-beaten truck. The victim was running for his life. Evil missed and plowed into the victim's truck. Evil backed up and circled for another strike. Evil spun and skidded through the parking lot several times, driving through a trash can and over the grass and bushes. Finally, Evil was on target and mowed the victim down with his truck, driving right over him. To my knowledge, witness accounts and evidence never confirmed exactly how many times Evil stopped, backed up over the victim, then drove forward over the victim again, but it was several.

All that time, the witness was on the phone with a 911 operator and he was still on the phone with her when I arrived. Why were we not given any more information when the call was dispatched or before we arrived on the scene? No one can answer that question, but it is an ongoing problem where I work. When all was said and done, there were at least five witnesses who watched the whole episode unfold. Two of those witnesses actually drove right through the melee as the victim was being beaten down in the parking lot in front of them. They did nothing. The only person who even called 911 was the victim's friend, who was watching the entire horrifying incident as it unfolded—but from a safe distance of course.

How's that for a real bunch of positive American role models?

CHAPTER THREE
Your Own Private Idaho

Awareness is a key trait in any Sheepdog. For years the law enforcement curriculum has included "color codes of awareness" (The concept of "Color Codes of Awareness" was first introduced by Col. Jeff Cooper, USMC retired.) that are used to refer to different states of mental alertness. The first color on the scale is white. When a person is "in the white", it means that they are virtually oblivious to their environment and their surroundings. They are relaxed and unprepared to deal with any type of threat that may arise. Someone who is in the white is most likely to become a victim, whether of blind circumstance or from a directed act of Evil. A person in this condition would not only not recognize an imminent threat, but when that threat materialized would be in no condition to respond to it in an appropriate or effective manner. Sadly, condition white is how most people live their lives from day to day. It's like the old song by the B-52s, "Living in your own private Idaho—underground like a wild potato." (The B-52s Private Idaho, 1980, Lyrics by Kate Pierson, Fred Schneider, Keith Strickland, Cindy Wilson and Ricky Wilson.)

Moreover, when a person who is "in the white" suddenly comes face to face with some type of threat (which could be anything from a roadway obstruction to an active assault) they are usually launched into "condition black", which is a state of sheer panic. All rational thought processes are abandoned to the irrational emotion of the moment and the person becomes a virtually useless and helpless victim of whatever circumstance he allowed himself to fall into.

All too often people who operate motor vehicles do so in condition white. We have all seen or heard of people who drive while applying make-up, talking on the cell phone, reading the newspaper, eating lunch, daydreaming or anything else that keeps their attention from the task at hand. Blind luck often keeps these people out of accidents but the law of averages usually catches up to them and they have an accident of some type.

One of the more amusing examples of driving "in the white" occurred while I was assisting in a house-moving detail. When a developer buys a piece of land that he intends to develop, if it happens to have a house on it, it is not at all unusual for either the developer or the original owner to sell the house and have it moved to a new lot. Because most houses are fairly large when compared to the average roadway, they need to be moved at times when traffic is light. That means that they often are moved at night.

The procedure for moving a house in our area is fairly simple. The person or corporation that is moving the house applies for permits to move the house through the various jurisdictions and provides the route along which the house is to be moved. Each jurisdiction has its own rules for issuing the permits and usually requires that at least two officers in marked cars accompany the house on its journey. One officer deflects traffic in the front and one in the rear of the house. There are also a multitude of support personnel in vehicles with yellow lights that surround the house as it moves along the roadway.

You would think that something as large as a house, which takes up at least four lanes (48 feet) of roadway, would be relatively easy for a driver to see, especially when the house is surrounded by flashing blue lights, blinking yellow caution lights, and miscellaneous flags and strobes. The driver of one vehicle in particular happened to be engaged in an argument with her passenger. She didn't have time to be bothered with paying attention to all of those pesky flashing lights, so she just drove around them. Once she maneuvered around the first police car that was frantically trying to divert her from the path of the oncoming behemoth, she steered around one or two of the support vehicles, sped up and slammed right into the front corner of the house that had since come to a complete stop in the roadway. Then she had the nerve to yell at us for allowing her to hit the house. Too bad it's not against the law to be driving under the influence of sheer stupidity.

While encountering a house in the roadway may be somewhat rare, it is significantly more likely that a driver will be faced with any number of other types of obstructions that are less apparent but can still do substantial damage. Probably the most likely type of obstruction would be another vehicle. It is amazing to me the number of people who drive on a limited access freeway, presumably at speeds of around 65 mph or more, who have some type of mechanical malfunction and then stop their vehicles right smack-dab in the middle of a lane of traffic without any effort to get the car off the road.

Even paying just a smidgeon of attention to the surrounding environment should alert even the dumbest of human beings that his car is slowing down through no action of his own and prompt him to start moving toward the shoulder. Nothing short of a catastrophic mechanical failure (like your engine falling out) should be an excuse for stopping in a lane of travel; yet it happens with startling regularity.

Add to the oblivious-driver soup some more inattentive drivers traveling behind the one who thought that stopping in a lane of travel was good idea and you have the recipe for a big bang. Oddly enough, most of these types of collisions occur on long straight stretches of roadway where there is very little excuse for not seeing the obstruction well in advance of the crash.

A weatherman from one of our local TV stations, who by all accounts is a fine, upstanding and intelligent member of our community and one of my favorite meteorologists, was apparently distracted in some way when he found himself in the aforementioned scenario. He was driving up a long straight stretch of a four lane highway and did not see the vehicle stopped with its flashers on in the left center lane. Without so much as a shadow of a skid on the pavement, he plowed into the ass-end of the stalled car at full speed. His full-size SUV was demolished and disabled.

Thankfully, no one was seriously injured but we did have to close the entire highway to move the patients into ambulances and clear the roadway of vehicles and debris. It wouldn't have been so bad except for the fact that right after the ambulances pulled up, we received notice via radio that the adjacent jurisdiction was pursuing two armed robbers in a stolen vehicle who were actively shooting at police while fleeing. I wasn't too concerned since they were on a different highway, but wanted to be safe rather than sorry so I went to notify the ambulance crew that the chase might be coming in our direction. I told them that on the off-chance that it did, it would be safer for everyone to stay put.

I no sooner finished that last sentence than I saw the police helicopter buzzing over some nearby trees. It was heading in our direction with the "Night Sun" illuminating something, presumably Evil, directly beneath it.

"Oh crap," I thought to myself as I looked at my accident scene and the fully obstructed roadway and then back toward the rapidly approaching, high speed Evil and his law enforcement entourage. At that point, there really wasn't a whole lot I could do in the ten or so seconds I had left before the chase would be on top of us, so I just yelled a final warning to anyone else on the scene who may not have seen the pursuit coming and dove for the shoulder of the road to take cover.

We had been warned that Evil was shooting at police from the car so I was taking aim on the car with my sidearm from behind the minimal cover offered by the steel guard rail. Evil managed to zoom through the accident scene through a narrow passage on the right shoulder. He flew within inches of me and the ambulance on his right and the rest of the traffic that had stopped for the accident on his left. I imagine that Evil was so preoccupied with navigating the accident scene and circumventing any obstructions that he didn't have time to shoot at us even if he had wanted to. We all breathed a sigh of relief as the pursuing police cars whizzed by us with no adverse effects other than a cloud of dust and a little rise in everyone's blood pressure.

Anyway, the point I am trying to make is that it is vitally important to remain alert while driving because you never know what might be lurking just ahead of you or right around the corner. The same may be said for everyday life. Being aware of your surroundings not only lets you see potential Evil ahead of time (and take appropriate measures to avoid or confront it) but it also sends a subliminal message to Evil that perhaps he would be better off picking another target.

When I had been on the police department for about four years, I was assigned to the evening watch (3:00 PM to 1:00 AM) and was often awake in the early hours of the morning. Such was the case one night at around 0230 hours when I decided to take my little dog (a pug named Dexter) to the ATM (ATM stands for "Automatic Teller Machine". We don't say "ATM machine" because that would be redundant.) and then to some late night drive-thru for a snack. We hopped into my mint condition 1963 Ford Thunderbird (I really loved that car) and headed for the bank just around the corner from my apartment.

I pulled up and parked directly in front of the walk-up ATM that was located in a fairly well-lighted shopping center. I immediately noticed three young males standing about fifty feet away. Staying true to Evil form, they were in a shadowy area that was between the bank and an all night breakfast joint. As if acting on cue in some poorly choreographed play, one of the males peeled off from the others and disappeared behind the bank building just as I exited my car. Those little alarm bells in my head were ringing more furiously than Quasimodo on a rampage, but I wasn't really worried as I slid my right hand under my shirt and gripped the ever so friendly grip of my Beretta, model 92, semi-automatic, Justice dispenser.

I nonchalantly glanced from side to side, eying first the two remaining males in the shadows and then the opposite side of the bank where I assumed Evil number 3 was about to appear. That little hint of a grin overcame my face as I started to think about what a bad day Evil was about to have. My pulse definitely quickened as time started to slow down noticeably. The two males to my right were now watching me with all the intensity of diehard baseball fans mesmerized by a tied World Series in the bottom of the ninth.

I remember glancing back to my left just as Evil number 3 broke the plane of the corner of the building heading straight for me. He was staring right at me and I was thinking to myself, "Uh-oh, here it comes." But alas, it was not meant to be.

I was just about to give Evil the surprise of his life when he made an abrupt about-face and went back around the corner. Simultaneously I noticed the glare of headlights reflecting off of the front of the ATM. Evil didn't know it but fate, in the form of another late night bank customer, had just saved his sorry butt from certain extinction.

I cautiously returned to my car and to my little dog who, in his puppy ignorance, was just happy that I had returned after such a long journey and not concerned with the implications of what had almost happened. I stayed in my car and watched the next ATM customer go about his business and laughed to myself that he was about as aware of the lurking Evil as was my pug. I also used the time to call dispatch on my state of the art, six pound, "portable" bag phone that was all the rage back then. They sent a couple of cars and after a protracted foot pursuit we were able to round up two of the three bad guys. One of them was later convicted in the stabbing death of an elderly woman that occurred at that same ATM. Both the bank and the breakfast joint have since been closed, only supporting the vicious cycle of poverty that is both caused and sustained by crime (not vice versa).

Now seems like as good a time as any to mention the other three color codes (since I know you are dying to know what they are). They are the antitheses to conditions white and black. They are conditions yellow, orange and red. These conditions are positive levels of awareness. Condition yellow is to be relaxed but also prepared and aware of one's surroundings, ready to deal with whatever threat may arise. That was the condition I was in when I approached the ATM.

"Orange" describes a state of alarm where someone who was in condition yellow has actually perceived a threat and is preparing to meet that threat with whatever force or action may be necessary. That was the condition I moved to after seeing bad guy number three head around the back of the bank.

Red describes the next logical step for the Sheepdog who has gone from yellow to orange and is now facing that immediate threat, fully prepared to meet it headlong and to defeat it by any means at his disposal. Through it all he maintains his awareness and control. That is the level I was about to be in (hopefully) if Evil had made one more move to try to victimize me.

I chose that scenario to illustrate the positive levels of awareness (and their almost natural progression) because it is one that any person could potentially find himself in. Evil is out there and if you are not aware, it could very well sneak up on you and ruin your day, and maybe even your life. There are numerous possible endings to that story depending on the players. I am always armed and have no problem defending myself in that manner. Some people do not have that luxury or do not wish to exercise that particular God-given, Second Amendment right. Those people always have the right to run away, scream for someone else to come and save them, try to negotiate with Evil or just give up as if there were some honor in being a victim. The opposite of victim is 'victor', and that is something I endeavor to be in every encounter with Evil.

I seriously doubt that any human being could maintain a condition yellow at every moment of their life. Even the best allows his mind to wander on occasion and can be taken by surprise, but those moments hopefully are few and far between, relative to the big picture.

CHAPTER FOUR
Nable's Four P's of Reaction Dynamics

There's an old axiom that states "action is always faster than reaction". Hopefully this concept is self explanatory. In a combat situation, he who is forced to react is at an obvious disadvantage because the person who is acting gets to go first. Therefore if you wish to gain and/or maintain the advantage, you must create a situation where Evil is forced to react to you.

In one of my physiology classes many moons ago, we were taught that the average person takes roughly 0.08—0.12 seconds (for an average of about 0.10 seconds) to make a muscle contract and relax. That is to say that to send the nerve impulse from my brain to a particular bundle of muscle fibers in order to have those muscle fibers initiate the chemical reaction that causes them to contract and then relax takes about 0.10 seconds. There was a simple test our professor had us perform to see if we were "average". He had us take a stop watch and press the stop/start button as fast as we could (twice) to see how much time elapsed. Since the clock wouldn't start until our finger muscles were fully contracted, a complete cycle would end when our muscle returned to the original state (which in this case was contraction). Most of us were within the 0.08—0.12 second time window.

Not too long ago I came across a study that tested simple reaction times in officers. (The "Tempe Study" conducted by Doctors Lewinsky and Dr. Bill Hudson.) In part of this study officers would react to a visual stimulus by pressing the trigger of a pistol one time. The average time that it took officers to complete the action once the stimulus was activated was 0.31 seconds. The act of pulling the trigger took actually 0.06 seconds (that was the time it took from when the trigger started moving until it stopped moving at the end of the pull) leaving 0.25 seconds for the officer to recognize the signal to pull the trigger and then begin the action of pulling the trigger. In this study, pulling the trigger was much like our old stopwatch exercise. To pull a trigger twice takes about .12 seconds just like pressing the start/stop button on the watch. If the average time to consciously cause a muscle to contract is around 0.10 seconds then that leaves about 0.15 seconds of processing time to react to a simple stimulus. In the same study, introducing a simple decision into the reaction doubled the response time in the average officer.

These times set a baseline of how fast such a reaction can be accomplished under simple and ideal circumstances. In the field, the object is to get as close to that baseline reaction time as is humanly possible, realizing that it is not likely that we will ever attain it. We all know that the more input a person's brain has or the more complex the decision, the longer it takes to process all of that input and the longer it takes for a given reaction to take place. It is comparable to overloading the RAM (random access memory) in you computer. The more tasks a computer (or a brain) is processing, the longer it takes to process them.

Consequently, reaction to very simple stimuli like a sound or a touch is likely to be much faster that reaction to a visual stimulus. By their very nature, our eyes provide our brains with much more input than a sound or a touch does. With more input, there's more processing time. When you add to that input, complex problem solving and/or emotions such as fear, anger, hatred, concern etc. then the brain's "RAM" gets more overloaded and more bogged down. Confusion is the natural result and the brain has to process all of that information to become unconfused.

Now, let's add to the RAM overload the effects of the fight or flight response (that we will discuss in a bit more detail in the next chapter). The fight or flight response is an emotional, right brain response that bypasses rational thought. Rational thought is one thing we need to formulate an efficient reaction. With all this going on in a person's brain, it's no wonder that poorly or inadequately trained individuals have trouble reacting properly, if at all, to stressful situations.

This is what makes training so important. It is also why I like to refer to police work as something you practice but never actually perfect. You should always be training yourself and practicing your art if you ever hope to be any good at it. You must also realize that you will never be perfect. Training isn't something that you do once or twice a year or when the boss signs you up for a class. Training is something you should do all the time, even if it means just practicing scenarios in your head. Training helps to shorten reaction times. It helps program some of the confusion out of your brain and hardwires certain actions and reactions so that they can be completed without actually having to think about them.

The dynamics of reacting can be broken down into four component parts. In my personal model, each component part of a reaction is a **P**. Each **P** represents a function that requires a specific, measurable, although unknown and case specific amount of time to complete. Training is the one thing that can help you significantly decrease the amount of time spent on each **P** and may even allow you to bypass some of the **P**'s entirely.

The first **P** in my model is Perception. Perception is the initiating phase of the reaction when the person who is doing the reacting receives the information that an action (that he is reacting to) has been performed. (Perhaps a more appropriate word would be 'reception', but that does doesn't start with 'P'.) Perception, in this context, is more of a mechanical function like hearing a gunshot or seeing some type of threat rather than a conscious realization of that action, which is more a part of the second P. Some may feel that processing is an integral part of perception. For those who wish to argue semantics, you may feel perfectly free to combine the first **P** with the second **P** into one big **P** which would, of course, reduce the number of **P**s to three. I, on the other hand, prefer to separate all of my **P**s—a luxury to which I feel I am entitled.

The second **P** stands for **P**rocessing. Processing is what the brain must do with the information that was perceived before it can move on to the third **P**. The processing phase is a very important phase because it determines the outcome of the entire reaction. Proper processing involves interpretation of the perceived action and the application of that interpretation via known models and subconscious filters. If the information regarding the perceived action is flawed or it is processed through the wrong models or filters, then the ultimate reaction will be flawed as well, much like that of the backup officer in the donut shop robbery/hostage scenario when he told dispatch that the first officer was fine even though she was in the custody of Evil. Processing is therefore a vital element of the training process.

The third **P** stands for **P**lan. Once the brain has perceived and processed the information regarding the action in question, it must take a measurable amount of time to formulate a plan to react to that action. This phase is also crucial in that the more training an individual does, the more plans he has programmed into his gray matter hard drive. Plans become more instinctual rather than cognitive and the conscious thought process is bypassed, in whole or in part, making the ultimate reaction time quicker.

The last **P** (if you haven't guessed by now) is for **P**erform. Once an action has been perceived and processed and a plan has been either formulated or selected from your hard drive to use to react to that action, then the last thing to do is perform…the plan, that is. The actual, physical performance of a particular act is something that training benefits as well. Obviously, the more you practice something, the better your body performs it. Such repetition leads to the development of "muscle memory".

In firearms training, we teach people to practice presentation of their firearm from the holster. With enough repetition, your muscles learn and remember where your pistol is located and how to get it out of the holster and point it at a target instinctively. This is the same process that, after years of practice, allows you to point your index finger directly at something you are looking at without having to stop and think about it, or to do other simple things we take for granted like throwing a Frisbee or catching a ball. Training also tends to link the planning and performing **P**s together transforming them both into somewhat autonomic responses.

To make the best use of muscle memory, you have to make sure that your equipment remains in good working order and is always located in the same place. Any time you alter your equipment you need to retrain your muscle memory which, depending on the individual, requires hundreds if not thousands of *correct* repetitions.

The next natural step in this progression is "tactics". Webster's definition of tactics is "The science of arranging…with reference to short-term objectives." (It is distinguished from "strategy", which implies a broader, long term objective.) A tactic (or tactics collectively) is something that is designed to make the act of reaching a particular goal as efficient and effective as possible. Having good tactics means having a sound reason for doing things the way that you do them. Tactics can be as simple as tucking your laces into your boot to prevent them from getting caught on something or coming untied at the worst possible moment, or they can be as complicated as clearing a building with multiple teams and multiple bad guys.

Good tactics are developed through study, experience and interaction with others who share your same goals and interests. Good tactics are implemented through training and practice. Tactics are constantly evolving and being refined by those who aren't afraid to ask, "Why?"

Good tactics force Evil to deal with the 4 **P**'s as often as possible. If circumstance happens to force us to deal with the 4 **P**'s, then hopefully our tactics will help us do so with remarkable speed and astounding efficiency. That is why we train.

In the following section I use traffic stops as an example of certain tactics and problem solving methods. It is a brief look at the subject that is only meant to illustrate the broader point.

3.2 It's Not A Sweater

While sitting in a restaurant one night, I was conversing with another officer about a class we had taken on vehicle pullovers. Early in the conversation we were interrupted by a young lady who was sitting in an adjacent booth. She had overheard part of our conversation and it sparked her interest. She was the kind of young lady who if you shone a flashlight in her ear it would make her eyes shine. She said something to the effect of, "I work in the fashion industry (Translation: first part time job at the trend shop in the mall.) and I think it's kinda neet that you guys were talking about sweaters."

"Huh?" We replied, stunned by the perplexing nature of the interruption.

"You know...pullovers."

It just goes to show that things can be interpreted in vastly different ways depending on who is doing the interpreting. We all have different filters that our brains use to process reality into our own unique perceptions. That is why perception (which is actually the processing part of my model) really is reality.

I hope the reader will keep this in mind throughout this chapter specifically and throughout this book in general. I am the product of my years of experiences which may have made my filters slightly different than yours. That fact makes my perceptions neither more nor less correct than yours; it merely makes them different.

While I could feasibly dedicate an entire book to the topic of vehicle pullovers, I want to offer some perspectives that may be a little out of the mainstream. In my career as a police trainer I have had the privilege of training recruits who have never been involved with police work on any level and I have had the opportunity to train veteran officers with years of experience. Each trainee brings with him/her a lifetime of baggage. Their baggage may be helpful or it may be a hindrance but one thing is for sure, it makes them all different in one way or another.

The biggest problem I face with new police officers is convincing them that Evil exists and that sometimes police officers have to be mean to do their job. The biggest problem I have with veteran officers is trying to get them to try something new.

Because of time constraints, only the most basic of traffic stop procedures are taught at our Police Academy. Sadly, there are many officers who never seek out any additional training and as a result, spend their entire careers performing every traffic stop the way that they were taught in the Academy. Doing so is much like going straight from a high school level driver education course onto the NASCAR circuit. It can be a recipe for disaster.

There are a few tactics that I like to teach my students that I will go over before getting back to the entertainment. As with many aspects of police work, I try to get my students to avoid the habit of getting stuck in a routine. When you do something the same way every time, it becomes somewhat of an automatic, unconscious action. To avoid becoming a victim and to tip the scales in his/her favor, a police officer must always be alert and thinking. Routines tend to numb our senses and make us predictable.

The old saying that no plan survives contact with the enemy is essentially correct. The plans that we practice are merely starting points from which we begin to improvise, act and react.

One of the first things I try to hammer into the heads of trainees is to always try to keep the primary weapon hand empty. Under extreme stress, people tend to focus on one action at a time. They tend to tense up their muscles and as a result, anything held in the hands is gripped more tightly. People under extreme stress also tend to revert to pre-programmed responses rather than consciously thinking through each action and reaction. There is no situation more stressful than fighting for your very life. Therefore, if you are holding something in your primary weapon hand when a life threatening situation unfolds, you are likely to hold onto whatever it is and you lose valuable reaction time trying to figure out why your gun isn't coming out of your holster like it's supposed to.

Keeping the weapon hand empty is not a new concept. One application of this concept where I see the most officers having difficulty is in the area of talking on the radio. The way most police cars are configured, the in-car radio microphone is generally used by the right hand. Most officers are right handed. Therefore, if you use the car radio and you shoot right-handed, your primary weapon hand is no longer empty. For that reason, I recommend that every officer practice using his/her non-weapon hand to activate the radio microphone and since that would make it difficult to use the in-car 'mike', I recommend getting into the habit of using the portable radio and activating it with the non-weapon hand.

I have seen officers on high stress traffic stops act as if they are glued to their in-car radio microphone. I have seen officers faced with a threat exit their patrol cars with their radio mikes still in their hand. If it weren't such a scary prospect, it would be laughable. Sometimes the officer is yanked back into the vehicle when he pulls the mike to the limit of its cord length. Other times the officer yanks the mike right out of the radio and takes it with him. In any case, his weapon hand retains the microphone and therefore cannot engage a threat with that weapon if necessary.

A somewhat more common response is that while waiting to give his dispatcher what he thinks is vital radio traffic, the officer will realize a potential threat and as part of the processing phase will throw the radio mike down to focus on the problem at hand. Then, when he comes back to the radio mike, he can't find it because he is programmed to pick it up off of its cradle and it is no longer there. Another frequent response is to grasp the mike tightly, pressing the transmit key thereby transmitting everything the officer is saying to the suspect. The simple tactic to avoid all of these problems and more is to use the portable radio whenever possible. It is more likely to be in the same place all the time, can be positioned in any number of convenient ways, and can be accessed by the non-weapon hand.

While on the subject of the radio, I would like to interject a somewhat controversial idea. That idea is that no matter what any trainer teaches in the police academy, a radio is not likely to have anything to do with saving an officer's life unless it is used as a blunt force weapon. We as trainers tend to overemphasize the importance of always broadcasting our situation and location over the radio before we do anything else. That mentality has gotten more than one officer killed.

Most deadly force encounters last only seconds. If backup is close enough to respond in those few seconds then hopefully you would not have to request it over the radio. If backup is not close enough to respond in those few seconds, calling for it could not possibly help the situation in any imaginable way. If you waste those few seconds trying to call for help, then you essentially have wasted your life. While you were calling for someone else to come and save you, you could have been acting to save yourself. If you can only do one thing at a time under stress, please let that one thing be trying to inflict as much damage on Evil as is humanly possible rather than simply making a recording for posterity of your last few terrified moments prior to becoming a name on a wall somewhere. You are far more capable of saving your own life than your radio is. You just have to have the will to do it.

Police officers often get stuck in a rut as far as traffic stops are concerned. Many officers see a violator, activate their emergency equipment, and then wait for the vehicle to stop before broadcasting anything over the radio in reference to the stop. The problem with this is that officers get conditioned to make the traffic stop and then sit there until there is enough time to broadcast all of the information over the radio at one time. Only then does the officer approach the violator. Meanwhile, the violator has had plenty of time to formulate a plan of attack, load his Uzi, hide his drugs, get his story straight with his passenger, arm his nuclear warheads etc.

The way I teach my students is to try to run a tag number (if available) before doing anything. That way, if the car is stolen or wanted the officer knows about it before making a stop and can take appropriate precautions. The next step is to pick a logical place to attempt the stop and give that information over the radio before activating any emergency equipment. The object here is that when the violator vehicle comes to a stop, the officer can focus 100% of his/her energy on the violator and the circumstances surrounding the stop. The officer should be out of the patrol car as soon as possible after the violator's vehicle comes to a stop. If the violator doesn't stop as planned, the officer can always update the location as time permits. If time doesn't permit, responding officers will at least know the officer's last location and direction of travel.

I have said before that no plan survives contact with the enemy. Sometimes Evil anticipates a traffic stop to 'get the drop on the officer'. Sometimes Evil continues to drive while formulating an escape plan. Sometimes Evil just plain does something totally unexpected. (The other option is a high speed pursuit which I don't intend to deal with here.) Sometimes the radio is so busy that there is no time to make a broadcast. The bottom line is that when the stop goes down, whether or not you have told anything to anyone, the officer needs to focus all of his/her attention on the situation at hand and contact the violator as soon as possible and control the scene (taking advantage of the four P's) to avoid being taken by surprise. If the officer doesn't feel comfortable making the stop without telling a dispatcher, then there is always the option of letting the violator go!

According to the FBI UCR statistics for the ten year period 1993-2002, 95 out 636 police officers killed in the line of duty by felonious assault were killed while making a traffic stop. That's roughly 15%. On average, about one third of the officers killed on traffic stops are attacked before they ever exit the patrol car. Of those 95 officers killed on traffic stops, 73 contacted their radio dispatcher prior to the assault. Those officers are still dead. Their radios did not save them. I would bet that in at least some of those instances, the radio was a contributing factor in the officer's death.

CHAPTER FIVE
Dah, Which Way Did He Go George?

I can't remember which cartoon it was, but as a child I remember watching one of those typical cartoon pursuits where the pursuer lost sight of the pursue-ee and all he could say was, "Dah, which way did he go George? Which way did he go?" It seems as though a large number of our inexperienced officers get that same sort of look when they lose sight of Evil in a pursuit, whether it is on foot or in a vehicle. I know that in my area, police officers are given virtually no training on how to track a bad guy.

In my book, "Searching for Evil and the Perfect Donut", I dedicate a chapter to foot pursuits and cover some basic behavioral patterns that are statistically significant when it comes to hunting down or chasing Evil. For those of you that have not read that book, I will take a minute or two to recap the highlights, and for those of you who have, consider this a brief review. I will then go on to cover some of the aspects of basic tracking that were not covered in the first book. 'Tracking' is a topic that is sorely under-taught in most police curriculums with which I have been acquainted.

I would like to qualify the following information by stating that it is drawn from my years of police work in a largely suburban area, which has a mix of residential, commercial, and industrial areas as well as areas of undeveloped land. The basic principles should remain consistent regardless of environment.

However, be cognizant that different environmental factors may affect Evil's behavior in a way that makes it seem as though he is not following the patterns when in reality he actually is. The patterns I discuss are by no means absolutes. They are simply patterns that recur too often to be ignored.

First, let's take a look at the fight or flight response. The fight or flight response is an innate self defense mechanism shared by most higher animals that causes some very unique things to happen to the body. Bear in mind that the basic purpose of this instinct is to create a condition of body and mind that will most effectually facilitate survival in an actual or **perceived** life or death encounter.

The process is initiated when the brain perceives a threat and stimulates the release of certain chemicals into the bloodstream. Many police officers refer to this as the "adrenaline dump".

The adrenaline dump causes several things to happen. First, the respiratory rate increases to allow for the intake of greater amounts of oxygen to fuel the muscles needed to engage in a fight or in flight. Blood flow to the areas of the body least likely to be used in the encounter (such as the digestive tract) is curtailed. In extreme circumstances the body will also evacuate the bladder and/or the bowels, perhaps to discard unneeded weight and to provide an olfactory deterrent to any would-be predators. Blood flow to the extremities, like fingers and toes, also decreases so that in the event of an injury to less vital muscles, there is little blood loss. Blood flow to major muscle groups is consequently increased since these are the muscles most needed to accomplish an escape or to engage in mortal combat.

One of the most important consequences of the fight or flight response is the loss of fine motor skills. Since the body shunts the blood away from the little muscles in our hands and the increase in energy causes uncontrollable shaking, it becomes very difficult to do simple tasks such as reloading a pistol or even holding it steady. Other tasks are nearly impossible, like finding the door key for your car or putting a key into a lock.

By its very nature, the fight or flight response completely bypasses the rational mind. The pupils dilate and our awareness intensifies. Fear becomes the dominating emotion. Irrational thought processes are the inevitable result. People just cannot think clearly when suffering the effect of the fight or flight response. The effects of this condition were perhaps best stated by the 18th century British statesman Edmund Burke, "No passion so effectually robs the mind of all its powers of acting and reasoning as fear."

Then we have what I call the "wounded deer" phenomenon. Many hunters will tell you that after they wound a deer, the deer will often sprint to escape immediate harm but then circle back around to familiar ground and perceived safety rather than running headlong into unknown territory. Usually, the circling seems to be to the right, or clockwise.

I think that most people have heard of the concept of "left brain" vs. "right brain". The left brain is logical, rational, objective and analytical. The right brain is more illogical, emotional, abstract and intuitive etc. The behavior exhibited in response to the fight or flight syndrome is more like that which is associated with right brain activity. Maybe I am way off base here (since I am not a student of brain physiology) but maybe this right brain behavior accounts for the abnormally high occurrence of right-hand circles in both animals and perpetrators that suffer from the fight or flight response. I guess it could also be a result of the Coreolis effect which would mean that Evil would turn left in the Southern hemisphere but let's not go there. Let someone else study that for a doctoral thesis or something.

Since the response in a fleeing perpetrator is fueled by much the same instincts as that of the wounded deer, the perpetrator will often not travel far before circling back to where he started. Since many pursuing police officers are suffering from a lesser degree (or no degree at all) of the fight or flight response, they often outthink themselves. They use their rational minds to try to decide where Evil went and they think that since it wouldn't make sense to run around in circles then Evil wouldn't do it.

The best way to catch Evil is to think like Evil. If Evil suffers from the effects of the fight or flight response then he is not thinking rationally and will do things that just don't make sense. As long as the pursuers remain cognizant of that fact, they can use it to their advantage.

In addition to a tendency for right hand turns, Evil tends to keep right when traversing open spaces or corridors and often gets more confused when forced by obstacles to make left turns.

Lastly, the fight or flight response causes the body to expend massive amounts of energy very quickly. Consequently, when the effects of the adrenaline begin to wear off, the body becomes extremely fatigued and must rest. If Evil thinks it is out of sight of its pursuers, then it would only be natural to assume that it would find somewhere to rest and recoup the lost energy. This often happens early on in a foot chase and is responsible for "Nable's 100 yard rule", which is based on the observation that most perpetrators tend to stop and hide within 100 yards of the last location where Evil thinks the good guys last saw him.

My intention over the next few pages is to show how to apply these behavioral characteristics and some observational skills and principles to the four levels of predation that an officer may experience in a foot pursuit. By predation, I mean that officers searching for Evil will inevitably be involved in a foot pursuit. The officer is the predator and Evil is the prey. As the predator, the officer will either be in hot pursuit mode, warm pursuit mode, search mode, or the tracking mode.

Hot pursuit is where the prey is visible and actively fleeing. Warm pursuit is where the officer is still hot on the trail but just far enough behind Evil to have lost sight of him. The tracking mode and the search mode are both employed when Evil has gained a significant lead or is hiding somewhere and the officer is not really sure which way Evil went. Whether officers use the tracking mode or the search mode depends primarily on the level of expertise of the involved officers and the amount of time and resources available to those officers.

Hot pursuit mode is really a no-brainer. You watch where Evil goes and you follow him. In hot pursuit mode, it has been my experience that you will still see the effects of the fight or flight response as outlined previously. Evil is generally panicked and running scared. It is not uncommon to watch Evil run headlong into a fence or a hedge when a simple course alteration of as little as ten feet would have put him on a path that avoided the obstruction entirely. If the environment permits, Evil will routinely make those tell-tale right hand turns.

One factor that may override the "wounded deer syndrome" is if Evil has a specific location in mind that he is running toward and/or has a specific knowledge of the area where he is running. It is not unheard of that certain perpetrators will instigate a foot chase so that they can lead an officer into a booby trap or an ambush. In this case, however, the standard rules of the fight or flight response do not apply because the situation is orchestrated and not random.

Similarly, if Evil is close to home or to his getaway vehicle, the only thing on his mind is getting to the perceived safety that those locations would offer. Again, the non-randomness of having a mindful destination overrides some of the fight or flight response characteristics.

While in hot pursuit mode, it is important to remember that the response is "fight or flight". If flight doesn't work, then look out for the fight. Evil can easily turn on its pursuer if it feels that capture may be imminent. Both parties will be drained after exerting the energy needed in even a short foot chase and when you're drained, your hand to hand combat skills will suffer no matter how good you think you are.

Human beings are instinctively "sight hunters". Just like most animals, when we chase something, we want to catch it with our hands. It may not be tactically sound to pounce on a perpetrator without backup. There's no easy answer as to what to do when you catch Evil, just be careful and use all the tools at your disposal as appropriate and necessary.

Warm pursuit is the middle ground between hot pursuit and tracking or search modes. Consequently it incorporates aspects of both. It may also be the most difficult of the three modes to deal with from a psychological perspective. You still have the adrenaline that goes with a hot pursuit but no outlet for it because you have lost sight of Evil. You have to relax quickly and concentrate on the clues at hand so as not to lose Evil completely if it can be helped.

When in doubt, employ some of the aforementioned theories to your warm pursuit mentality. Carefully look at the physical characteristics of the surrounding environment and try to look at them from the perspective of your prey. At night, perceptions are greatly altered by lighting. If Evil doesn't have a way to see in the dark, then you should view the environment in the same way before deciding on a course to follow.

Now seems as good a time as any to introduce a couple of tracking terms. "Sign" is a term used to refer to something that is evidence that a moving body leaves behind when it traverses through a particular area. This evidence can be as obvious as a footprint or tire track, or a subtle as a turned over rock or broken leaf. In one instance where I was tracking Evil that had fled on foot from a traffic stop at night, I stopped and turned my light off to view my surroundings as my prey would have. It was on the ground in front of me that I saw a unique "sign" indicating that someone had recently passed where I stood. There was the obvious glow of a crushed firefly in the pinestraw at my feet. Anyone who has ever crushed a firefly knows that once they are dead, their light doesn't shine for very long. I knew I was on the right track and had to be very close. If I hadn't turned off my light, I would have missed that vitally important clue.

The second term I want to introduce is "jump tracking". Jump tracking is essentially finding an obvious sign (like a big fat footprint) and then moving on quickly in the direction indicated by that sign until you find the next sign. This is essentially what happens in warm pursuit mode. You follow in the last known direction of Evil, keeping in mind the characteristic behavior of the fight or flight syndrome, and then you start jump tracking. If this does not lead you to Evil then, if time and manpower permits, you revert to the most tedious and time consuming of the four modes which is the tracking mode.

I would like to add here that I am not holding myself out to be an expert in tracking and I will be the first to admit that my level of expertise in the matter is based solely on years of trial and error, and no formal training in the subject. It seems as though there are a lot of books that emphasize how to track people whether they are lost or they are trying to avoid detection when the tracker is unencumbered by many of the restraints suffered by the average street officer. These books generally focus on the true art of tracking which requires an enormous amount of time relative to what the average law enforcement officer may have in a given hunt for a particular bad guy. There seems to be very little work done covering the types of "hunts" that the average patrol officer is likely to initiate or be a part of on a given shift. I hope that I have had enough experience that I can pass along some information that may fill some of the gaps in police training that exists in the area of tracking down bad guys.

True tracking involves finding the last visible sign left by your prey and then meticulously hunting for each and every step that you can find in the hopes that the trail will lead you straight to Evil. To effectively track something or someone you must learn to look for clues (sign) that are not as obvious as a footprint or a tire track, but are more indirect evidence of movement.

One of the most obvious but often overlooked clues for nighttime tracking (and sometimes daytime) is dew. Grass is a great place to find dew prints. Sometimes they are barely visible and can only be seen with light from a certain angle or from some distance away. Dew is condensation on plant leaves that in nature forms fairly uniformly on the tops of exposed plants. When you step on or otherwise disturb the dew, it leaves a mark. The marks usually appear dark since light is reflected by the water and not reflected by the areas where the dew has been knocked off. I have been on numerous manhunts where officers are running around in a random manner in the dark with flashlights a blazin' trying to find a bad guy. They will waste valuable time searching a yard or field where there is lots of dew on the ground and no dew prints—which means no Evil. Similarly, a brief inspection of the area often turns up a highly visible trail if the officer knows what to look for.

Any number of things can constitute "sign", but I will touch on some of the more obvious ones which I encounter regularly. Spider webs are awesome indicators. If you are tracking someone and you run into a spider web, it's a good bet that the person you are looking for didn't pass through that area. Unless he was crawling or flying, he would have to run into the same web you did. (Take into account the height of Evil vs. the height of the web also.)

Fences almost always have some sort of clue on them if Evil went over. Look for dew or water. If the fence is wet with dew, look for areas where the dew has been smeared or wiped off as an indicator of a crossing point. If the fence is dry, look for wet areas possibly left by a sweating Evil. Wooden or painted fences often have marks from Evil's shoes or may even be dented or broken from Evil's frantic flight into or over them.

Almost all vegetation leaves some sort of sign. The heavier the vegetation usually means the better the trail to follow. Plants naturally grow upward and their leaves face the sunshine. The presence of upside down leaves or flattened stems generally means that something has altered their natural state.

Soil can be scraped, flattened or turned without leaving an obvious footprint. Dirt is naturally amorphous and uniform in its surface appearance. Flat spots indicate an unnatural force has been applied to the surface. Scrapes also constitute visible sign that is often seen in slopes or embankments. Also, soil often retains moisture just below the surface and if it is disturbed, the darker, moist soil may appear on the surface for a time until it dries out. This is "sign". Remember, when looking for sign in different environments, to test the soil or ground cover periodically. Put your own foot down or run through the woods and see what kind of sign you leave. Break a stick or press down the grass to see what it looks like. That's how you learn.

The way that the tracking mode differs from the search mode is that in the tracking mode you are searching intently for sign in a defined and identifiable trail. Tracking is tedious and may take a considerable amount of time. In search mode you are merely conducting a standard and hopefully patterned search which may turn up sign that points to a trail or may turn up the actual target of the search. Search mode is also what is reverted to by inexperienced officers who do not have the experience or the desire to track. Search mode is the crudest and often least effective of the four modes and has a tendency to destroy the most evidence. Search mode may, however, be more effective if you have lots of searchers coupled with very little time. The search mode is most effective when the object of the search is contained in a defined area. At that point there is no need to track because the location of the target is essentially known.

I am sure that if I wanted to, I could list sign for hours and bore you to death. Instead, I want you to think about all the sign that can be left by prey and even go try to find some on your own. Then share your findings with the people you work with so everyone can get on the same page. I am going to get back to telling some stories now.

A call came out at an apartment complex of a home invasion robbery. The apartment was on the fourth or fifth floor and radio advised us that Evil had entered via an unlocked balcony door and had left the same way. About five officers responded and saturated the area rather quickly. We came up with nothing early in our hunt which caused me to switch to plan B. If Evil did not live in that apartment building, then he had to have left some sign as he departed.

I chose a tactic that has proved itself valuable countless times when an initial, cursory search has produced nothing. I picked a nice dark spot to sit and wait. If Evil got scared by someone or something, he would likely hide until he felt safe to proceed. Just as all the other officers left the immediate area, I heard a crackle in the woods nearby. He was a lot closer than I had dreamed possible. Evil was right next to the ground floor apartment underneath the one he had just robbed. He was lying (not laying) down in the thick ivy that grew underneath the trees. He was too close for me to risk talking on the radio but too far for me to initiate a surprise attack on my own. To reveal myself meant an instant foot chase and I really hate those. They take so much energy and those darn bad guys are usually younger, faster, less encumbered by the weight of equipment, and far more motivated to escape capture than I am to do the capturing. So I watched.

He passed less than 20 yards from my location thinking he was in the clear. He headed up the embankment toward a side street that separated that apartment complex from another. When he crossed the street, I could see him lie (not lay) down in the woods on the other side. That was when I called out that I had the subject in sight. Before I could give directions to my fellow officers on how to surround him, one rather zealous unit came running up the well lighted street right toward Evil.

That was enough to spook Evil and switch everyone involved into hot pursuit mode. Evil jumped a hedge and fence into the adjacent apartment complex and ran through the parking lot straight toward the fence in the rear. I chose a flanking maneuver to try to keep Evil in sight and be the designated radio man, directing any units that were still on the way. The primary pursuit officers then did not have to take time and mental energy to do anything other than stay hot on Evil's trail.

There was a thick band of woods and a row of houses in Evil's path before he would get to a street that ran perpendicular to his course of flight. I stayed on the roadway that was parallel to his path and as a result could pass that band much more quickly. I got to the next street way ahead of Evil.

I positioned myself in the dark waiting to see him emerge from the row of houses on my right. A few moments of anxious waiting proved fruitful when Evil, as expected, emerged and crossed the street I was on. The only problem was that he had remained somewhat true to the fight or flight response principles and had worked his way to his right, which was, coincidentally, in the opposite direction of me.

Instead of being closer to Evil I was farther away and the primary pursuit officers had run out of energy. We regrouped on the street where I had last seen Evil cross and switched to warm pursuit mode.

Even though there was a good distance between Evil and me when I saw him last, I was able to gauge his crossing point by using a mailbox and a streetlight as reference points. I knew that he had passed within the confines of a particular yard so I had one officer go one yard to the far side of that yard, one officer to check the target yard, and I went to the yard on the near side of the target yard. (That's a lot of yards.)

We trampled through our respective yards and regrouped on the backside of the row of homes. I had found no "sign" and neither had the other two officers. I was a bit frustrated because I knew I had seen him. I backtracked and started checking the other yards and in doing so was able to find a clear trail that one of the other officers had missed.

The officer had gone down the driveway where I was sure Evil had gone but he made one tiny error. He was using his flashlight and in doing so was able to see a large drop-off at the end of the driveway that was not at all illuminated. What he did not think of was that Evil had no flashlight and therefore could not have seen that same drop-off. Consequently, there was a distinct dent in the dirt at the bottom of that drop-off, undoubtedly where Evil had taken a comical spill.

Just beyond that dent was a small expanse of good ole southern fescue before a large patch of liriope. (Liriope is sometimes called monkey grass and is that thick, low growing, wispy, evergreen grass that grows almost everywhere in the Southeast.) Right through the middle of the liriope was a very plain trail that was actually more visible from ground level than it was when illuminated from the driveway above it.

At the end of the trail in the grass was a small picket fence. The picket fence had a nice fresh broken slat that pointed to Evil's last direction of flight. Unfortunately for us, we were running out of time and resources and we had to terminate the search. The home invasion was ultimately revealed to be a lover's quarrel between two men.

During our informal debrief of the situation, I made sure to razz the officer that missed such an obvious trail. That is our way. We don't mean nuthin' by it.

My next story that incorporates a bit of tracking started with a call from a female who was involved in a dispute with an ex-boyfriend. The caller allegedly had a restraining order against the man who was at her apartment. He was refusing to leave. Under Georgia law, if the caller indeed had a restraining order, then his mere presence at the location constituted the felony offense of aggravated stalking. As is often the case, no further information was available.

The apartment complex where she lived was relatively large. The buildings were placed about the property in a manner that I am sure must have made sense to the architect, but to no one since. Even though I had been in that complex countless times in my sixteen years on the street, I still had difficulty locating the correct building.

By process of elimination, I knew that I was nearing the correct building. As I made the final turn that would put me at my destination, I saw several people standing in the parking lot. It was only a few seconds before one of the individuals in the crowd, a young, thugly looking man wearing "felony high-tops", baggy shorts and a T-shirt draped over his shoulders, realized that the police were coming. He took one look at me and took off running in the opposite direction.

My remarkably astute powers of deduction told me that there was a distinct possibility that the guy who ran was likely Evil. I grabbed the radio mike to let dispatch know simultaneously that I was on scene and that the suspect had just taken off on foot. (That's what we in the business call posting a "bushbond". In other words, the only thing he left behind as a surety to guarantee his appearance in court was the bushes.) I gave a brief description and direction of travel as I pulled up to the remaining members of the parking lot congregation. The "victim" ran up to my window. She was visibly shaken and with an all too familiar whimper in her voice she pleaded with me to go after the man who had just run away. She told me that it wasn't fair that he kept harassing, threatening and intimidating her and "always got away with it".

I assured her that I would do my best to facilitate his timely capture and drove off in the direction he had gone. At that particular time, several other units were working another, higher priority call involving a fight with weapons and then another call on a burglary in progress. Since I was not actually in active pursuit of my suspect, I called my backup unit to the tac channel to give him further directions. By going to the tac channel, I would not interfere with any emergency transmissions from the units on the fight call or the burglary call.

I told my backup unit that the suspect was wanted for aggravated stalking (among other things) and repeated the description. I told him the last known direction of travel (which was toward the entrance to the complex). I also told him that I would be searching for Evil on foot. In my mind, I assumed that since I had said that I would be on foot, the backup unit would stay in his patrol car. I should not have assumed. Assumption is the mother of all screw-ups.

I went to the area where the suspect was last seen to begin the search. I saw no evidence of his trajectory but I did see a resident sitting in her car. I asked her if she had seen anyone run by and she pointed in a direction consistent with his last known line of travel.

I followed the invisible path between two buildings, across the parking lot and to two more buildings. I knew that most of the time fleeing Evil makes right turns and tends to circle so that's what I did. I carefully checked the area and made my right turn.

I was going slowly so as not to overlook a hiding Evil or to walk into an ambush by a waiting Evil. It wasn't long before I saw Evil about a hundred yards ahead of me creeping through the shadows between two other buildings.

I was still on the tac channel and I raised my backup unit. He responded and I told him that I had the suspect in sight and gave our location. Since the search was now an active following and would likely soon escalate to a hot pursuit, I switched my radio back to the main channel.

I broadcasted, "128 to radio, I have the suspect in sight. He's heading northbound between buildings 14 and 15 and is heading back toward the river." His current course was exactly 180 degrees from his original course. Whether by chance or design, he was circling back to his starting point.

I did my level best to stay hidden from him in the shadows while endeavoring to keep him in sight. I knew that his twenty year advantage added to my twenty pounds of extra clothing and gear would make it nearly impossible for me to win an outright foot-race with Evil. If I wanted to catch him, I had to outsmart him.

He again made a right turn down the main driveway of the complex. He was trying to stay in the shadows close to the buildings to keep from being seen. He had no idea that I was following him.

Enter the unknown variable. One of our police officers lived in that complex and took his patrol car home with him every day. He parked that car by the leasing office of the complex. That just so happened to be where Evil was heading. I told radio that Evil had made a right turn and was heading for the leasing office at a slow jog. I thought for sure that my backup unit would come storming in our direction in his patrol car and we would get the drop on Evil.

If my backup unit had stayed in his car, I am sure that's exactly what would have happened. Unbeknownst to me, he was on foot as well and was a long way off.

When Evil saw the parked patrol car by the leasing office, he thought that it was accompanied by a police officer and he made an abrupt about-face. Before I knew it, he was coming back at me full speed. I tried to stop him but the element of surprise was lost and the foot race I had so desperately tried to avoid, was on.

He ran straight through the parking lot back toward one of two exits from the complex. I tried to take a shortcut between some buildings but ran into a natural barrier. I had already blurted out over the radio that he was running and had given his direction of travel. The radio was unusually quiet.

As I was navigating a route around the aforementioned barrier, I remember saying on my radio in an increasingly impatient tone, "Radio, are there any units in the area that can assist?"

All the dispatcher said was, "Negative."

Normally, I try to remain calm and professional on the radio but was a bit irritated due to a combination of my current predicament and the fact that that particular dispatcher had a long history of poor performance. My sarcastic response was (I quote), "I'm clear on no back-up on the foot chase with the felon."

The dispatcher matched my tone and snipped back, "128, Radio was not clear. You did not declare a foot chase."

In all my years I had never thought that a foot chase was something that had to be "declared". I thought declarations were made when you started a new country or changed mental or marital status. My last smart-ass comment was, "Radio, I've been chasing this guy for twenty minutes! Where have you been?"

Even though it had only been about five minutes, I figured that the exaggeration might help get my point across. Almost immediately, the radio came to life with all sorts of units asking for my location etc. About then, I ran around a building and into the officer who lived in the complex. He asked what was up and I told him in winded bursts what was going on as I continued my feeble attempt at the game of catch up.

That particular officer was a few years younger and, since he was about 75% legs, he was a lot faster than I was. I was glad to have him join me. We both proceeded in the direction where Evil was last seen as I used the radio to direct the some eight or so backup units that had materialized in and around the complex.

I directed a unit to stand by at the entrance/exit that was near where Evil was running. I requested some units to assist on foot while others took strategic locations either on foot or in their cars. We began a methodical search of the area (switched to "search mode"), applying the aforementioned pursuit principles as our guide for where to do the searching. We were looking primarily for Evil since we had a fairly good idea of where he was, but we were also looking for sign that might indicate his direction of travel or precise location. I knew that if Evil hadn't gone into an apartment, he would not enjoy his freedom for much longer.

Our search was winding down as we grew near to the entrance where officers were standing by. All that was left to check was a narrow band of woods (about fifty yards long and twenty five yards wide) between one of the buildings and the roadway.

Wouldn't you know, Evil was hunkered down in the thickest part of those woods. As a number of uniformed and plain clothes officers converged on his position, he began to "resist". He was dragged, kicking and screaming, from the woods. He was proclaiming his innocence (as Evil always does) and demanding to know what the charges were. He kept saying that he was just walking to a friend's house when we jumped him for no reason etc. etc.

Stupid little Evil kept digging his hole deeper and deeper until I decided to reveal to him that I had been following him and then chasing him through the complex for quite some time. Of course his only response to that was "Not uh."

After all that trouble and the subsequent fifteen hours we had to guard him at the hospital, the court dropped the aggravated stalking case because, surprise, the girlfriend didn't come to court.

There was one other noteworthy item to mention along the lines of "sign". After the Evil was apprehended, I was debriefing with one of the other officers at the scene. He had been stationed at the exit of the complex near where we caught Evil. He mentioned that he felt we were on the right track initially, because as he was sitting dark in the roadway, he saw a family of opossums come out of the woods and cross the road near him.

Animals can constitute sign when their behavior is abnormal. Wild animals are fairly astute and would not have left the safety and cover of the woods so near a human without a reason.

5.2 Path—Finder

My next story is one of my all time favorites. It involves an officer whom we all kid (perhaps a little too much sometimes) because he has a little "attention deficit disorder". He also tends to over-dramatize things sometimes.

He and another officer were on their way to a suspicious person call. Our radio dispatcher, in a very uncommon display of competence, had actually gotten a fairly decent description of the perpetrator's vehicle. The lookout was for a gray, Nissan Pathfinder. Wouldn't you know it, while enroute to the call, one of the officers saw a gray, Nissan Pathfinder leaving the area. Thinking that it was a little too much for coincidence, the officer made a u-turn to try to catch the vehicle. Evil, in his likely state of guilt-induced paranoia, saw the police car turn around on him and launched evasive maneuver number one. He sped up, meaning to turn onto a side street, but in his fight or flight confusion he missed the intended road and turned into the driveway of a commercial business instead.

Evil was stuck and the primary officer was not far behind him, blocking the only viable exit for anything as large as a motor vehicle. By the time the first officer pulled up and stopped behind the truck, Evil had already abandoned it in favor of attempting an escape on foot. The situation dictated that it was time to enter tracking mode, since no one had seen exactly which way Evil went. The second officer on scene was Corporal

Attention Deficit Disorder (not his real name) and he promptly launched into a three minute soliloquy trying to direct about ten officers to set up a perimeter. That wouldn't have been so bad except for two reasons: It took way too long for all the direction without any time given up for anyone else to talk on the radio, and we only had about four officers to respond.

I was the third car to the scene and when I got there, Corporal ADD was still in mid soliloquy. I walked right past him and went straight into tracking mode. The area where the truck had been abandoned was flanked on the right by a high wall, in the front by a steep embankment and dark woods, and to the rear by a wide open space where the first officer would have seen Evil in had Evil been there. That meant in all likelihood, Evil went left.

To the left was an open parking area for about fifty feet or so. Then there was a small wood line before another commercial property. There was a storage house to the right of that area so that's where I went first. There were some wooden pallets or some such thing on the back of that storage house and close inspection revealed the remnants of a dewy footprint. I was jumptracking in that direction when I found a few more obvious prints and then hit another wood line.

I checked to my right first and saw a small dirt road or driveway so that's where I headed. I got about twenty feet or so before I realized that the ground was fairly soft and I was leaving the only visible footprints in the area. Convinced that he did not go that way, I backtracked.

I picked up the last visible footprint and stayed heading in that direction, which was essentially straight along the rear property line of all the businesses there. Evil was not turning because his terrain was corralling him down a fairly narrow path behind all the buildings.

I jumptracked to another obvious footprint that led down to a culvert where there was some heavy mud. I could see some obviously fresh tracks in the mud but also noticed that another officer had made his way in front of me. I stopped so as not to add any more confusing tracks to the trail and called to the officer ahead.

"Did you walk through all this mud?" I asked.

"Not me, I went around. I didn't want to get my boots dirty."

"Those tracks have to be Evil," I thought to myself. I followed them straight through the slimy thick mud about forty feet or so until I came to a break. There was a nice clean concrete slab behind a building and on it were some gorgeous muddy footprints. I got that little smile I always get when I'm about to execute a surprise pounce on Evil. The mud tracks led straight to a big metal dumpster.

I used hand signs to communicate to the officer behind me what I had found. I quietly circled the dumpster to make sure that he hadn't gone out the other side and saw no other tracks. I positioned myself on one door to the dumpster and the other two officers had now converged and were on the other side. I was to be "cover" and they would be "contact". I flung open the steel door to the dumpster and there was the frightened, muddy Evil. I yelled a couple of choice expletives and the second dumpster door opened as Evil was violently extracted from his not-so-clever hiding place.

By the time I made it around to join the contact team, he was already cuffed.

"Nice of you to hide with the rest of the trash," I said smugly.

We jerked him to his evil little feet and started walking him toward the road. I swear that I am not making this up. We ran straight into the headlights of the trash truck that was there to empty the dumpster. Only a few minutes of lag time and he would have been on his way to the dump. Darn.

5.3 Blood Trail

I will polish off this chapter with a similar story that involves jumptracking Evil in a situation that was almost too good to be true. For once, Murphy's Law was working against the bad guy. It started when Evil broke into his estranged girlfriend's apartment, hell-bent on exacting revenge for some perceived wrong that she had done to him or to his ego.

When he smashed through the window of the apartment in his drunken rage, he managed to cut himself pretty severely on one of the shards of glass. By the time he untangled himself from the mini blinds, his girlfriend was already on the phone with 911. He got about one smack in on his ex before he figured it was time to scoot before the cops got there.

When I got to the scene, I got a quick rundown on what had transpired. The female told me that Evil had moved out of the apartment recently and that she was pretty sure that he lived close by in a house he had rented, but wasn't sure exactly where the house was. A cursory check of the area of the broken window revealed a minor blood trail. Since it was probable that Evil was headed back home and he had left a visible trail, I immediately went to work trying to track him.

Blood trails are an interesting thing to try to follow. Fresh blood is a lot easier to see because it is bright red. The longer it stays on the ground, the darker it becomes. Usually, a minor injury will quit bleeding after a short amount of time which means that that aspect of the trail may disappear. For more significant injuries, the wounded person may try to bind or cover the wound to prevent blood loss resulting in the same loss of the trail. This guy, probably as a result of his intoxication, was bleeding enough to leave a good trail and never tried to cover it up.

Once I established his direction of travel, every few feet or so I found a nice bright red droplet. This trail was probably easier to follow than "dumpster boy" but it took a little longer because Evil lived about a half mile away. He had a destination in mind and took the shortest route he knew to get there.

His bright red trail led through some light woods and across a two lane roadway toward an area that had only three houses. On average I would say that there was at least one good droplet every eight feet or so. The trail led to one that at first glance I though was abandoned but as I worked my way around the back, I found more bloody evidence of his presence going right up the back stairs.

I banged on the door of the house and an old woman answered. She tried to pretend she didn't know what I was talking about when I told her I was after Evil. When I threatened to lock her up for obstruction and showed her the obvious blood trail, she reluctantly let me in. The last sign I saw was a smear of blood around the frame to the attic crawl space.

After a few idle threats into the dark void of the attic, Evil called out that he was surrendering. The whole exercise took less than twenty minutes.

I hope that this chapter has not only been entertaining, but if you work in law enforcement, I hope you have learned something that will be useful in the search for Evil. The most important thing for people to remember is that we function best when we work as a team. Civilians are our support personnel and we need their help to do the best job we can. The officers on the front lines have to share tactics and information with each other and those who work together need to train together.

CHAPTER SIX
The Big Red Hump

Somewhere around the year 1990, officers in several levels of our department were concentrating at least some of their efforts toward locating the perpetrator of several homicides and a few other, not quite so Evil, drug related crimes. Like most Evil, he wasn't very smart. Even though he had to know that he was a wanted man, he continued to be seen frequenting the same general areas in which he had committed his homicides. We were close to getting him several times but because of luck, Murphy's Law, or that guardian angel/demon that some perpetrators seem to have regularly intervening on their behalf, he always managed to stay just beyond our grasp.

Whether as an act of frustration, desperation, or some other –ation, the powers that be ordered several detectives, a couple of "special units" (not the kind that have their own Olympics) and a couple of regular beat officers to conduct 'round-the-clock surveillance in an apartment complex that our Evil was known to frequent. (As an interesting aside, it was on that detail that I discovered that the local pizza place would actually deliver a pizza to the woods.)

Anyway, we were all taking turns watching this apartment complex when word came out that Evil was possibly spotted in a four door vehicle with several other fine, upstanding, pillars of the community. We quickly orchestrated a plan for a takedown on the car. When we got the word from one of the undercover units that Evil was on the move, we pounced.

With surprising fluidity of movement the suspect's car was surrounded on three sides by a multitude of marked and unmarked cars and a barrage of blinding lights from every possible source we could muster. Once we were fairly certain that the car was not going to try to flee, the primary unit began initiating standard felony stop procedures. The first command he directed toward the car full of Evil was for all the occupants to place their hands on the interior roof of the car. He ordered them, in no uncertain terms, to remain perfectly still until specifically told to move.

We began the tedious extraction procedure for the driver and, at some point during the process, at least a few of us noticed that the passenger in the left rear seat was moving his right hand from the ceiling of the car toward his lap.

"Passenger in the rear, put your hands up. Do it now!" screamed the primary officer over the public address system.

Whether as a result of fatigue, defiance, or sheer stupidity, he moved his hand back to the ceiling very slowly, rather than with the rapidity you would expect from someone facing imminent reprisal for failure to comply. Once it was back in the proper position he was admonished that should he feel the need to move again without receiving instructions to do so, his movement would be considered an act of aggression and would be dealt with severely.

It was not very long before that same right hand, which incidentally is the weapon hand for the majority of people in this world, came back off of the ceiling and down toward Evil's lap. Just as the primary officer began to bark at Evil to once again put his hand up, a shot rang out from the crowd of police. The back windshield turned almost opaque as it shattered into little tiny pieces that were still held together by the plastic that makes safety glass safe. The bullet that shattered the windshield also pierced the right shoulder of the obstinate young Evil.

Despite whatever pain he had to have been in, he sat as still as a stone statue in the back seat of that car, with both hands pressed hard into the ceiling of the car. It was as if the Epoxy Fairy had come and cemented his hands to the headliner while no one was looking. It is amazing what human beings can accomplish with the proper motivation.

Now, the point to this story is a simple one. After thinking through that situation countless times over the years I realized something that may, to some, sound at the very least, controversial. What I am about to postulate will certainly cause the multitudes of pansy-liberal-pacifist-sissies to cringe, wince, grimace and cry aloud. That realization was that if police officers in this country actually shot every one who they were justified in shooting, there would be a helluva lot more folks getting shot by the police every single day: So why aren't they?

The answer is, "Because of The Big Red Hump." Before I can explain exactly what The Big Red Hump is, though, I have to go over a few other things.

Force is something that every officer routinely uses in the performance of his/her duties. After all, the word 'force' is right there in our job title; Law En**force**ment. Force can be as negligible and innocuous as the officer's presence, or it can be more overt like a full-blown fist fight. These types of force are not really that controversial or out of the ordinary most of the time. In essence, officers are accustomed to using force in varying degrees. Generally, they do so with no malice and are completely justified.

Deadly force, however, is different animal all together. Rarely does the average officer have the opportunity or necessity to use force which is intended or likely to cause death or great bodily harm. Deadly force carries with it a plethora of implications that are political, religious, psychological, moral, racial and who knows what else. Because of all of the potential implications and ramifications involved with the deadly force option and because deadly force is something that has a ring of permanence, many officers have difficulty in using it.

The fact is, that in use of force situations like so many other situations, perception is in fact reality. The only thing that matters in a departmental inquiry or in a court of law is what a reasonable officer in the same situation would have perceived. We sometimes discover after the fact that our perceptions were wrong, but that does not and cannot be a factor in the post-incident evaluation, whether it is by the officer's peers, his department, a court of law, or a civilian mob.

The standard, three pronged test for the application of deadly force is that the officer using that force perceived that Evil had the ability (i.e. a weapon of some type capable of causing death or great bodily harm) to inflict deadly force on the officer or a third person, that Evil had the opportunity to inflict deadly force on the officer or a third person (using the weapon) and that the person that would be Evil's target had to actually be in jeopardy of receiving harm from Evil if Evil decided to take advantage of the ability and the opportunity.

A baseball bat is a deadly weapon and would be considered "ability". A baseball bat in Evil's hand would add "opportunity". "Jeopardy" would exist when Evil was close enough to use that baseball bat to inflict deadly force on someone. An officer does not need to wait for Evil to actually hit someone with the bat before he can take positive action. Hopefully the basic philosophy is clear. Please remember that a perception is all that is required. If that perception is later proven erroneous, it is still a non-issue. We cannot second guess ourselves and when deadly force is perceived, the intended target of that force must respond, there are no do-overs. We can't wait to see if we are going to die to be justified in defending ourselves.

Now, let's consider the aforementioned scenario. The officers had stopped a suspected murderer/drug dealer. He was known to be armed. He was surrounded by police who told him not to move. He moved. He reached with his right hand toward a location where most people carry firearms and he did it twice. Both the department and the court system agreed that the shooting was justified. I have heard some people disagree with that and I ask them, "At what point do you think the officer should have fired."

The inevitable answer to that question is something like, "They should have waited until they saw a gun." Let me tell you from experience that I can fire a gun from inside of an automobile with a surprising degree of accuracy without ever putting my firearm where anyone outside the vehicle would be able to see it without x-ray glasses. Car doors or body panels rarely, if ever, stop bullets. Engine blocks and wheels are about the only place on a car that is regularly thick enough to prevent penetration of even small handgun rounds.

If a police officer tells you to do something, I recommend that you do it. You can complain later if necessary, but failure to comply could be dangerous, or even deadly. You have no way of knowing what that officer thinks (perceives) that you may have done. You may match the description of the world's most wanted, serial cop killer. The fact that you aren't will have no bearing in the use of force hearing after you have been shot because you failed to obey the officer's lawful commands.

That being said I would like to comment on the officer that actually did the shooting discussed in my anecdote. He had a very distinguished military career before joining the police department. He was a very down to earth, decent guy. He wasn't mean or angry or hateful but he also wouldn't take any crap from anyone. He knew what he was allowed to do, when he was allowed to do it, and he did it without hesitating. Over the course of his career, he was involved in thirty-four shooting incidents. Most of them resulted in the death of the target Evil. None of them were even remotely suspicious. (This officer was on active police duty prior to the Tennessee vs. Garner decision.)

The classic, 1976 John Wayne movie entitled, "The Shootist" is one of my favorite films. It was John Wayne's last movie and definitely one of his greatest. The movie has a couple of quotes in it which represent an insight that is quite uncommon in the Hollywood of today and that are pertinent to the current discussion. The lead character is J. B. Books (played brilliantly by John Wayne) and his ever-eager, protégé/wannabe Gillom Rogers (almost as brilliantly played by Ron Howard). After Books grants young Gillom his wish for a shooting lesson, Gillom beams as he comments that his "spread" on the target is almost as tight as his hero's.

"How'd you ever kill so many men?" Gillom marvels of Mr. Books.

"I've lived most of my life in the wild country. You set a code of laws to live by."

"What laws?" young Gillom asks.

"I won't be wronged, I won't be insulted, 'n I won't be laid a hand on. I don't do these things to other people. I require the same from them."

"How could you get into so many fights and always come out on top? I nearly tied ya shootin'."

Truer words have never been spoken than in J. B. Books' reply. "Friend, there's nobody up there shootin' back atcha. It isn't always being fast—or even accurate that counts; it's being willing. I found out early that most men, regardless of cause or need, aren't willing. They blink an eye, or draw a breath before they pull the trigger. I won't." ("The Shootist", Starring John Wayne, Paramount Pictures, 1976)

Neither would that officer.

There are two reasons why officers do not employ the deadly force option more often than they do. One reason is that some people, no matter how dire the situation, are psychologically incapable of doing anything that will threaten the life of another human being. The second reason is that for whatever reason, just like J. B. Books said, officers hesitate. Most of the time, that hesitation turns out to be a good thing and deadly force is not required, even if it had been suggested or even recommended. Sometimes, however, that hesitation can prove fatal if a gunfight is inevitable, meaning that deadly force was in fact required and no other option would suffice.

I have created a model that I use to try to break down the deadly force encounter into easy-to-understand elements. The first part of Nable's deadly force spectrum is the blue area. (Please don't confuse these "colors" with the color codes of awareness discussed elsewhere in this book.) I use the color blue because it is the color of "cool". The blue area is where deadly force has not yet presented itself as an obvious option. That is where most officers are or should be on a regular basis. Since officers are always armed, any confrontation they enter into is, by definition, an armed confrontation. An officer always has to be aware and ready for a deadly force encounter should it materialize, but at the same time, cannot go around with gun in hand, challenging every person that he meets as if they are armed felons. (That reminds me of a quote I hear repeated often in our business, "Be polite. Be professional. But have a plan to kill everyone you meet." I have no idea who came up with this quote but if I did I would tell you here.) Therefore, an officer, or for that matter anyone who carries a firearm for self-defense, must be confident and prepared, both physically and psychologically because after all, that is the definition of "cool".

At the point where deadly force begins to loom as a possible outcome of a given encounter, the officer moves to the gray area. I chose the color gray to describe this part of the spectrum because gray is the natural transitional color from any other color into or out of the color black. In the gray area the officer is aware of a potentially life-threatening circumstance where one or perhaps two of the three elements of a deadly force encounter are present, but not the third. (i.e. ability and opportunity but not jeopardy)

The next phase is black. I chose the color black because of its obvious implications. Black represents the unknown and is a longstanding trademark of Evil. The black area of the spectrum is the phase where all three elements exist, whether in perception or in reality, since they are one in the same, but there is still no active assault on the officer. In other words, there is a bad guy who is reaching for a weapon but he has not yet used it, or a bad guy who has a gun that he is in the process of deploying but hasn't actually fired it yet. Once the move has been made into the black area of my spectrum, deadly force on the part of the officer is completely justified but deadly force has not actually been physically implemented against the officer.

It is here that I would like to present (finally) the idea of the Big Red Hump. The Big Red Hump is a psychological stop sign. I chose the color red because it represents something that demands attention, like a stop sign. Red also contrasts brilliantly with the color black. It can be different for every person (and can be anywhere across the entire use of force spectrum depending on the individual) but it seems that for the average officer the Big Red Hump is somewhere in the middle of that black area. For some people, the Hump may be small while for others it is monumentally huge. For some people, The Big Red Hump is insurmountable while a select few on the opposite end of the scale seem to be genetically deprived of the hump all together. Of course there are also those whose humps are somewhere in the middle of these extremes.

Nonetheless, The Big Red Hump is something that anyone in a deadly force encounter must get over before he or she can actually use deadly force. It is that stopping point that is created by any number of mental factors discussed previously. It could be the inherent aversion to taking a life. It could be the philosophical insecurity that comes with liability training or an incomplete understanding of deadly force options and applications. It could be a combination of these or any other number of mitigating factors. To decipher all the components of a person's Big Red Hump is something I could never hope to accomplish. That is a function that lies within the purview of doctors and academics that study such things. My only hope is to make people understand that the Hump exists.

The idea for anyone who has the will to survive is to get over that Big Red Hump before ever being involved in a deadly force encounter. That is what the John Wayne character was talking about. Once the Big Red Hump has been dealt with, you will not hesitate. The result is that you may actually shoot someone that didn't really **need** to be shot but you will never shoot anyone that you were not justified in shooting, providing that you understand and comply with the rules of ability, opportunity and jeopardy. Just like John Wayne's character, you will not hesitate and, hopefully, you will always come out on top.

Almost every officer I know has been in at least one situation where deadly force would have been justified but was not employed. It is the nature of our job and the nature of the average officer. The vast majority of officers are Good people and really don't want to hurt anyone. One situation that arises in training quite frequently involves weapon retention. As part of the weapon retention class, officers must defend their weapon against the assault of fellow student(s) bent on taking that weapon from them. We teach that should the officer be able to break away from his assailants, he should draw his weapon and prepare to fire. Inevitably, a student will ask, "Why am I taking my gun out of the holster? Won't that make it easier for the bad guy to get it from me?"

The reason is simple. If the bad guy makes one single solitary move toward your weapon, you shoot him.

"But how can I shoot him? He doesn't have a weapon?" The naïve always seem to ask.

What should be obvious is that Evil is making an overt attempt to get a weapon and you cannot afford to wait to see if he is going to be successful. To put the situation into context, I change some of the elements for the students.

Imagine that Evil is in a room with you and on a table situated between the two of you is a pistol. Evil looks you dead in the eye and says, "I am going to kill you." He then slowly starts to move toward the pistol. When he is within arms reach of the pistol you are in the black phase of Nable's deadly force spectrum. You are in a situation that is the very definition of ability, opportunity and jeopardy yet Evil has not actually fired a shot at you. You scream warnings at Evil but he continues to advance toward the weapon. Any time between now and the time he shoots you dead, you are justified in using deadly force. I just hope the Big Red Hump is not so large that it cannot be successfully circumnavigated. Legally, the officer is not required to run away although it is sometimes a viable option…especially if the Big Red Hump is too big.

The first situation is no different from the second. By assaulting an armed officer of the law and trying to get that officer's weapon, Evil is in effect saying, "I am going to kill you." If the situation allows the officer to present that weapon and Evil advances on it a second time, it is no different than if Evil were reaching for the gun on the table. The overt act of reaching for the gun (if he is close enough to be a threat) puts the officer into the black phase. The officer is completely justified in shooting even though no weapon is in Evil's possession...yet.

The final phase in my deadly force spectrum, if the encounter goes that far, is represented by the color white. I chose the color white because that is allegedly the color of the light which a person sees immediately after death...

How's This For A Hump?

One of our officers was working an auto accident on a busy highway near a private driveway. The private driveway wound off into the woods a considerable distance. The house it belonged to was not visible from the roadway. While the officer was working the accident scene, the homeowner arrived and drove around the wreck to go to his house. A few moments later, the homeowner was speeding back down the driveway toward the officer's location.

"Officer, officer, I need your help. There is a burglar in my house!"

The officer dropped what he was doing and hurried up to the house in question, followed by the homeowner. By that time, the house was visibly in flames. A figured appeared near one of the doors to the house and began walking toward the officer and the homeowner.

"I have no idea who that guy is," shouted the homeowner, implying that the stranger was likely the burglar/arsonist.

The officer drew his sidearm and challenged the stranger using some standard cop saying like, "Stop! Police!"

The stranger did not respond to the presence of the officer or to the officer's commands. At some point, he picked up a large metal paint bucket and began steadily advancing toward the officer with a blank look on his face.

The officer continued to scream at the suspect, but still there was no response. The suspect kept advancing.

"Drop the bucket! Freeze! Stop! Police! I really mean it this time!..." Who knows what the officer actually said but I am sure it was similar to the above. No matter, the suspect ignored him and kept advancing.

The officer was paralyzed (by the Big Red Hump) in his own tracks and before he knew it, Evil was upon him. Evil grabbed the officer's gun and was able to wrench it free from the officer's grasp with seemingly little effort. In the blink of an eye, the officer found himself staring down the barrel of his own gun.

"I'll give you three seconds before I start shooting," was the only thing that Evil said.

The officer turned and ran away. As promised, after the three seconds had elapsed, Evil started shooting. The officer's guardian angel must have been working overtime that day. Despite the fact that the officer never wore a bullet proof vest to work, the only injury he sustained was a glancing blow to the back from a ricocheted bullet.

Evil was apprehended without incident later that day.

The previous story may seem a bit outlandish to some but I can tell you with certainty that situations nearly identical to that one play themselves out with startling regularity. Sometimes the officers are not so lucky.

Now, let's break down the important elements of what

transpired. A citizen/homeowner reports a burglary, possibly in progress. This information is taken at face value since there is nothing to indicate that it shouldn't be taken that way. The option should always be present in the evaluator's mind that the information may be false or may only be a partial truth.

The officer goes to investigate accompanied by the reporting party. The reporting party sees the suspect and identifies him as someone who should not be there, hence he is possibly Evil. There is still the remote possibility that the reporting party is not being truthful but you can only act on the information you have at your disposal.

The next important point is that when challenged, the suspect does not respond. He advances toward the officer and has a metal bucket in his hand. Even if the suspect is deaf, the sight of a uniformed police officer pointing a gun at you should be enough to make any rational person stop whatever they are doing. The next logical question is whether or not a metal bucket can be a deadly weapon. The answer is, "Why of course it can be." If you disagree with that assessment then I will offer to hit you in the head with a metal bucket as hard as I can and we will see if it causes great bodily harm. Just because Evil's weapon may not be as refined as a handgun, if it is potentially deadly then that is all that counts. Equality of weaponry is not a variable in the deadly force equation.

So far we have the ability and the opportunity. As the gap between Evil and the officer closes, jeopardy becomes the final issue. When Evil is close enough to be a threat with his chosen weapon, then jeopardy exists and the officer is in the black phase of my deadly force spectrum. That is when it is OK to use deadly force against Evil. If the officer finds that he or she cannot get over the Big Red Hump, then there had better be a plan

B. Like Captain Taylor commented in the introduction to this book, sometimes the test comes before the lesson.

The officer's response to Evil in this situation is actually a fairly common one for people who have not yet successfully dealt with the Hump. I see it in training all the time. Officers are quick to pull their pistols and shout, "Stop police!" but they never mentally get past that point. They don't have any plan for what to do if the person doesn't stop as ordered. They seem to think that their gun and badge provide them with irresistible powers of mind control and when the mind control doesn't work they have a mental meltdown.

I can only assume that it is a condition due, in whole or in part, to the "it won't happen to me" frame of mind. That is a frame of mind that is all too common among "good" people. They tend to refuse to believe that there is any Evil out there and as long as they are good people, no bad will come to them. Because they are not mentally prepared to confront true Evil, even when it is staring them dead in the face, they slam head first into the Big Red Hump and get knocked silly. The Hump, for these people, cannot be overcome.

The officer in this story had a painful and frightening introduction to the Big Red Hump. At least he lived through it. The sad thing is that it seems as though he learned nothing from it. After the incident, he still would not wear a bullet proof vest to work and still would not carry a back-up weapon. It is my assumption that he never really accepted what happened to him and never dealt with it on a personal level, but only he knows if that's true.

CHAPTER SEVEN
The Best Laid Plans...

Sometimes it doesn't matter how well you may think you have calculated your surprise attack on Evil because sometimes fate just works against you. There is an incident that comes to mind that in retrospect is really kind of comical, but at the time really pissed me off. It is something that happened to me while I was working one of those off-duty security jobs in a shopping center. The management had hired police officers to work the complex from 6:00 PM to 2:00 AM every night of the week to help curb the incidents of vandalisms, thefts and fights that were driving away patrons and angering tenants.

It was around 10:00 PM when I noticed a suspicious looking "perp vehicle" riding around the parking lot with no apparent destination. My first impulse was that the four occupants of the vehicle were either looking to steal a car or, at the very least, to steal from one. I found a fairly well concealed spot to watch them from. I watched and waited. They backed into a dark part of the parking lot and one or two of the occupants exited the vehicle and began rearranging something in the trunk.

After a few minutes, they got back into the car and started driving around the parking lot again. This particular parking lot had two levels. The upper level was connected to the lower level by a long ramp that ran along the edge of the property. When I first set up surveillance on the suspected Evil, they were in the upper parking lot. After rummaging through their trunk, they exited out of a driveway on the opposite side of the property from where I was and then re-entered the property in the lower parking lot.

I was going to be real sneaky and decided to use that long ramp as my surveillance point because I could look out over the edge and see through some Bradford pear trees that, in all likelihood, would conceal me from Evil. There were only two vehicles parked on the ramp. One was a large SUV and one was a sedan. They happened to be parked next to each other so I took up a position between the two to watch the lower lot where Evil was.

I watched as Evil drove slowly through the lower parking lot, traversing line after line of parked cars that were potential targets. They passed nearly every car in the lower lot as they got closer and closer to the area where I was. I kept chuckling and thinking to myself how great it was that if they broke into a car, I would be literally right on top of them.

But much to my surprise, they passed the last row of cars beneath me and turned to make their way up the ramp that I was on. They were coming straight at me and the only place I had to hide was on the ground in front of the two cars that were parked next to where I was standing. Naturally I chose the larger of the two, the SUV, and sat down sort of underneath the front of the truck and up against the little ramp wall that was between me and the lower parking lot. I figured I would just sit there, out of sight, until they went by and then resume the surveillance operation.

Imagine my surprise when I realized that their target vehicle was the SUV I was hiding under. I watched as the car crept slowly up the ramp. One of the occupants got out and started looking around. He began walking up the ramp closer to my location while the car he had been in drove slowly right behind him. Because of my vantage point I could see only tires and the feet of Evil until he got close to my position. As he moved even closer, I could tell that he was looking around. He paused for a minute and made his final approach to the SUV. As soon as he got to the driver's door he saw me.

I think he was stunned with disbelief as he caught a glimpse of my uniform. I knew I had been seen so I had to make my move. As I scrambled out of my hiding place and greeted the would-be car thief I said, "Hey what are you doin'?"

Of course I got the usual response of, "Nuthin'," as the bad guy turned around and briskly walked back toward the car where his Evil friends were waiting. At some point, the car had turned around and was now heading the opposite direction. I tried closing the gap between me and Evil but as I moved faster, so did he. The last thing he said before he jumped into the moving getaway vehicle was, "I'm just waitin' to see a movieeeeee". The tires squealed as they exited onto a side street.

I was able to radio the vehicle description and a complete tag number to the on-duty units that were already on the way to my location. Unfortunately, to borrow a line from the old TV show 'Get Smart', we "missed it by that much."

There happened to be a rash of thefts from vehicles in shopping centers all around my location that night. A small consolation was that they didn't get anything from my parking lot. I am reasonably sure that the guys who ran from me were the ones who had broken into all those other cars. In all probability, the items they were rearranging in the trunk were the fruits of their previous crimes and they were just making room for more. Oh well. You win some—you lose some. That's the nature of the game.

To balance out this little chapter, I would like to include an interesting anecdote where fate actually worked against Evil instead of for him. It started when a fairly frantic call came into the 911 center around midnight. The caller was a man who told the operator that he had just shot someone. A few preliminary questions revealed that the caller was a bank guard who had gone to an office building to service an ATM. While he was working on the ATM, someone tried to rob him. He shot the bad guy and ran away from the scene to call the police.

When we arrived at the scene, the guard had had time to calm down somewhat. He directed us into the building where the alleged crime had occurred. What we found surprised everyone, including the guard. There was a woman, dressed in dark clothing, lying (not laying) on the floor. She had a bullet hole in her chest and was obviously quite dead. The guard was visibly shaken and confused. We ushered him back outside to try to get an idea of what had happened.

The following is as close to his account as I can recall:

"I got a call from the monitoring center that the ATM had gone down. All these machines are monitored and when something goes wrong with them, an alarm goes off and they dispatch me (or someone else) to fix the machine. When I got here, I went inside the building and opened up the machine. As soon as I got the machine open, a man came up behind me and told me not to move. He stuck something in my back that I thought was a gun. He told me that it was a robbery. I went for my pistol, turned around and fired. I saw the guy fall down with a gun in his hand. He was wearing a ski mask. I don't know what happened to that woman or where she came from. This doesn't make any sense."

Our first impulse was to think that, since it was late at night in an empty office building, maybe the woman just scared him and he shot her by accident and then concocted the robbery story to keep from getting in trouble. The only problem was that, unlike most people who are not telling the truth, he was sticking to his story and it was the same every time he told it. He wasn't showing any of the classic signs of deceit.

The case was at sort of a stand-still until we got a rather peculiar call from a man who wanted us to go check the address where we already were to see if we could locate his wife. He was supposedly worried that she had gone to use the ATM at that building and had not yet returned. Needless to say, our detectives were anxious to talk to him.

To make a fairly long investigation short, the detectives arrived at his house and in the driveway was the couple's car. As they approached the house they casually looked inside of the vehicle and made note of the black ski mask that was visible on the back seat of the car. During the interview, the man was obviously nervous and, unlike our bank guard, was showing all the classic signs of deceit. It took very little time to discern what had actually happened that night at the ATM.

One member of the husband and wife robbery team was a former employee of the bank. They had access to a telephone or computer linked code that would shut down the ATM remotely. They used the code to shut down the machine, knowing that the bank would dispatch someone to repair the problem. The plan was to wait for the guard to show up to fix the machine and rob him when he opened it.

They didn't think he would fight back and weren't prepared for a gunfight. In the adrenaline rush of the moment, the guard had suffered a common plight of anyone under the effect of extreme stress; he had tunnel vision that caused him to focus on the threat he saw (the gun that was actually in the hand of the masked woman). When he fired his weapon, he was completely unaware of the other person who was there (the male robber whose voice he had heard). Since he only saw one person, he thought that the person he shot also must have been the voice that he had heard talking to him. He was wrong. After the shooting, both the guard and the man (the remaining robber) were so scared that they fled the scene in opposite directions.

After the guard ran away, the man ran back to check on his wife and found her dead in the hallway by the ATM. He took her pistol and her ski mask and then he ran away too, trying to think of a way to cover the crime while lamenting the loss of his loved one. He didn't think long, hard or well enough and was ultimately convicted not only of armed robbery but also of the felony murder of his own wife. Felony murder is simply causing someone's death in the process of committing a felony.

Judging from what I saw, the jail time was irrelevant to Evil. He really loved his wife and his real punishment was losing her. Oh well, when you play with fire, you just might get burned.

CHAPTER EIGHT
Here We Go Again

Since everybody loves a car chase—sorry, I meant to say vehicle pursuit,—I figured that I would put a few in here for your enjoyment. I debated with myself over whether or not to put this first one in here because it is an admission on my part that I too once suffered from a strong case of "rookie-itis".(Rookie-itis is a well known disease that afflicts many young officers. Its causes are largely genetic in nature and the only known cure is experience.)

I had been a cop for about a year or so and was working on the 3:00 PM to 1:00 AM shift. I had just finished with my shift, had turned in all my paperwork and was walking through the parking lot to my personal car, ready to head home. We did not have the luxury of take-home radios back then so the only way I could hear what was going on was by listening to the car radio of one of the officers who was loading his patrol car, preparing to go on shift. I overheard the dispatcher saying something that wasn't so uncommon back then but now is nearly unheard of: "All units—be advised that Alpharetta PD is in pursuit, southbound on Roswell Rd. approaching the precinct."

There was a collective "Yahoo" from all the officers in the parking lot except for me. All I could think was, "Damn. I don't want to miss this one."

Everyone was scrambling to put the last of the necessary items into their patrol cars as one by one they peeled out of the parking lot. In a move that would make any police administrator shudder and cringe, I ran to my personal car and headed out to join the pursuit. (This was not the 1963 T-bird, it was a 1985 Lebaron GTS with high flow injectors and an aftermarket, high performance computer chip.) I realize that my actions then were nothing short of moronic, but I couldn't help it: I had the fever and it was burnin' bad.

I squealed out of the precinct parking lot behind the last of the marked patrol cars and just after the pursuit had zinged by us at about 100 mph. One thing that sticks out in my memory is the raw rumble and awesome throb of the savage power plant in Evil's late sixties muscle car (a 1969 Camaro). It was a stark contrast to the much tamer, more civilized, emission-controlled hum coming from the engines of the police cars that were hot on Evil's tail.

I wasn't too surprised that the little turbo-charged engine I had in my personal car was more than adequate for the task of keeping up with the pack. I turned on the interior light in my car so that any of the officers in the pursuit would be able to identify me. I also turned on my flashers to let people know I was participating. What I hoped was that any of the officers in the chase who happened to notice me would think that I was a detective in an unmarked car.

Evil headed straight for the interstate, which gave us all plenty of room to fall in behind him. I didn't have a radio so I hadn't yet learned that the reason we were chasing him was because he was wanted for armed robbery. My little car was in considerably better shape than most of the police cars that were in the pursuit. It handled better and had more on the top end than the cop cars, which turned out to be a bonus and a burden.

The average speed of the chase on the highway was between 110 and 120 MPH, a speed which my car could easily handle. However, some of the patrol cars were having trouble so I ended up passing quite a few of them before I noticed that I was almost at the front of the line. That was a position that even in my rookie-itis induced delirium I knew I didn't want to be in. I eased off the accelerator and moved over to the right to try to fade back into the long line of cars behind Evil.

We were moving into unfamiliar territory as we went from I-285 to I-20 East, heading toward the inner city, where Evil was likely going to try to run for it on foot. He tried to exit on an off-ramp somewhere in a run-down part of town. It was there that he had to face the reality that even though he could violate all the laws of man on a whim and flee to escape the consequences, he could not violate the laws of physics without receiving immediate adjudication and punishment without appeal for his transgression.

The Camaro slid off the roadway, down an embankment, over a drainage ditch, up the embankment on the other side and into a tall chain link fence that sought to protect a peaceful graveyard from the turmoil of the living world. The car finally stopped after pushing the fence about three or four feet inward. As is customary, Evil evacuated the vehicle and leapt over the fence like some steroidal gazelle.

A swarm of sheepdogs covered the car almost instantaneously while a few of us used the car as a ramp to run over the top of the fence and into the graveyard. Despite our valiant efforts, Evil faded into the darkness and eluded us that night. He was captured later without incident I am told. After admitting defeat to myself, I tucked my tail and got back in my car; hoping to leave unnoticed before anyone who cared (like a supervisor) got there.

I was lucky that nothing bad happened as a result of my lapse in judgment. I had plenty of time on my long ride home to reflect on what I had just done. Rest assured that too many lessons to list here were learned and I think I matured significantly that night.

8.2 Alone Again

My next chase illustrates several of Murphy's laws in action. Hopefully there is no need to point them out. It started like most chases do; abruptly and without warning. I was patrolling the main drag on a quiet night in the wee hours of the morning when a Jeep Cherokee, filled with malcontents, turned across my path out of a neighborhood that I knew was full of mostly elderly people.

I made a u-turn to check them out and they tipped their hand right away. They jammed on the gas pedal and so did I. Any doubts I had about their intentions evaporated into the moist spring air. It had just started to rain lightly which made high speed driving all the more treacherous. Still, I was determined to stay with them as long as I could—without exceeding my own limitations of course.

I had called for assistance almost immediately but none was available. I told radio to notify the adjoining jurisdiction that we were on the way, hoping that I might get some help from them. We started around the perimeter highway and were fast approaching the next jurisdiction when radio told me that help was on the way. I was a little relieved as I passed the Cobb Parkway exit and saw a Cobb County marked unit with his lights on moving to intercept.

That unit must have underestimated our speed because we blew by him like he was standing still. I watched my rear view mirror intermittently as his lights faded out of sight.

"Alone again," I thought. "Oh well. That's the way it goes."

We sped down the highway to an exit that I knew only by

name. I felt that same fleeting feeling of relief when I saw that Evil was exiting and that there were flashing blue lights standing by at the top of the ramp to keep traffic from flowing across our path. I was grateful for that little bit of assistance but really hoped that one of the cars would follow along.

No such luck. I found myself navigating surface streets at ridiculous speeds, in an unfamiliar area, pursuing a stolen car full of Evil in the dark and in the rain. I actually managed to call out street names as we passed and kept a fairly good chronicle of our movements up to the point where we turned down a very small, unmarked street. Moments later, Evil ploughed through a yard and got stuck in the mud. Staying true to form, all the vehicle's occupants spilled out into the night and, to further complicate matters, each fled in his own unique direction.

I actually started after one of them but several yards into the woods I realized that I had no idea where Evil went, and furthermore, I had no clue where I was. I trudged back to my car and had to take consolation in the fact that at least I had recovered the Jeep with no major damage. I later learned that the truck had been stolen from the house on the corner where I had first seen it turn in front of me. It was one of those rare times when the police were in the right place at the right time.

8.3 Rookie is as Rookie Does

This next case also involved a Jeep Cherokee. It all started one morning while I was patrolling in my usual state of high alert. Since I was the only car on the road, it wasn't difficult to notice when another car was coming toward me. I slowed down to watch for evidence of Evil as the vehicle passed by me going in the opposite direction.

Evidence of Evil was exactly what I saw. The absence of glass in the small, fixed, rear vent window suggested that someone had probably broken into that vehicle recently. While not definitive proof of anything in particular, it did warrant a little closer inspection.

So as not to spook the driver in the event that he was doing something that could earn him a free stay at the Gray-bar hotel, I watched in my rear view mirror as he did something that I half expected. He put on the brakes for a few seconds as if he were watching me in his rear view mirror, and then he turned off the main road onto a side street (right turn of course).

I immediately cut down an adjacent side street to intersect the road he was heading for. It didn't take long for me to catch sight of him. I had gotten his tag number when he passed me and was waiting for radio to give me the results of the NCIC check. I practice reading tags in the mirror just to see if I can and I have gotten fairly good at it.

I kept my distance from my prey until the tag check came back.

"Do you have that vehicle?" radio asked in a tone that told me that something must be up.

"That's affirmative radio." (That's a fancy way of saying yes.)

"Be advised that it shows signal 52 (stolen)."

"Received. I'm following it south on Glenridge Drive, heading toward Interstate 285."

A second unit responded over the radio, stating that he was close and was starting for my location. He knew that I wouldn't try to stop the vehicle until I had at least one other car with me so I didn't feel the need to say anything else.

"He's getting onto I-285 west."

Even though only one unit had called out on the radio, I had a pretty good feeling that everyone else was on the way unannounced. That's just the way we do things. The only thing that matters is that you go where you are needed, not that you tell radio. The radio needs to be quiet so that the officer involved in the situation can call out without fear of interrupting or being interrupted by a bunch of guys saying "I'm on the way too."

We continued down the highway and I updated our position over the radio. Evil still wasn't sure that I was behind him or that I knew his car was stolen. All pretenses dissolved, however, when a police car appeared out of the blue with lights and sirens blazing.

"Who the hell is that?" I thought to myself as Evil stomped on the gas and the chase was on.

The radio, which until that moment had been calm and quiet, burst to life with the overstressed voice of the only rookie on the street that night. He obviously hadn't been briefed on the proper procedures for surprise attacks on bad guys.

Oh well—what can you do. We were joined by the officer who had originally acknowledged that he was enroute to my location. The two of us naturally fell into standard vehicle pursuit mode, which meant that he would be the lead car and would run his lights and siren and would not say anything on the radio. I would be the second unit and would be responsible for all radio traffic and would therefore run with lights but without a siren.

No one knows what the rookie was thinking as he blew by both of us and got right on Evil's tail. There are plenty of reasons why rookies do that and many more why they shouldn't which I cover in detail in my first book, Searching for Evil and the Perfect Donut. (It's really good. You should read it.)

I knew from past experience that trying to get the rookie to back off would be an exercise in futility so I just concentrated on the task at hand. We pursued the stolen SUV around the perimeter highway. The interstate had no traffic so there was very little danger in the pursuit—very little danger except for the rookie who actually drove his car up next to the bad guy and started shining his spotlight on him. That wouldn't have been quite so bad if Evil had been in a lane other than the left lane, which put the rookie driving next to the median wall in the narrow emergency lane.

Rookie is as rookie does. Evil taught him a valuable lesson when he abruptly exited off the highway at the last possible moment. That tactic left the rookie driving down the interstate by himself since he couldn't react in time to make the exit behind Evil.

I saw that the SUV was heading up the exit ramp at ridiculous speeds so I called in that we would be canceling the pursuit. All emergency equipment went off and we watched as Evil continued up the long ramp with no regard for the approaching intersection. Just as he hit the intersection, he also hit the right rear quarter panel of a taxi causing a horrendous crash. The whole front end of the Jeep caved in as its rear end spun around to its left. The taxi spun several times clockwise as well and was essentially destroyed. Fortunately, the taxi driver emerged unscathed but obviously shaken.

As my competent backup officer and I pulled up to the scene we saw Evil leap from the Jeep and run straight for the grove of pine trees that grew in the triangle of land between the road we were on, the Interstate, and the entrance ramp that was on the other side of our exit ramp.

The first officer ran into the trees after Evil and before I got to them, he had laid the smackdown on the bad guy and had him in cuffs. As is so often the case with scumbag, maggot, criminals, he kept saying, "Ya'll got the wrong guy. I wasn't in that Jeep! It wasn't me! It must have been a guy that looked like me. I was just out for a walk when you guys tackled me." Blah blah blah.

The real sad part about this whole story is that the "rookie", though new to our department, allegedly had twenty-some years of experience working for a police department somewhere in New York.

8.4 Good Things Come To Those Who Wait

Sometimes, just because you find the fruits of Evil, doesn't mean you have to act right away. Occasionally, the officer who is really out to catch Evil will use things like that to his advantage. I was actively searching for Evil one night in one of our high crime areas when I saw a car come into the complex behind me and then make a quick evasive maneuver behind some buildings. By the time I got turned around and headed in Evil's direction, I noticed four suspicious young males. All them were walking in different directions and judging from their trajectories, they had all probably started at the same place…like the car I was looking for.

I only had to look for about two seconds before I saw the car in question. I knew that if they were up to something, the best I could hope for was to catch one of the four. Then, somehow, I would have to prove that he was in the car, which might have been extremely difficult. Instead, I opted to let them slide that time. They vacated the area pretty quickly and I circled around the block to go investigate the car. (If they had seen me go check out the car, then they probably would not come back to it.)

I ran the tag and it came back to a different car. I quickly wrote down the VIN and drove away to a more secure area to check it for stolen. Surprise, the car had been reported stolen a few days earlier. I decided to let it sit for a day or two to see if I could catch someone in it. It took just under twenty four hours for my plan to pay off.

The next night I was sitting in a parking lot across the

street from where the car had been parked. I looked up and there was what looked like the car driving right by me. I put my car in gear and headed after it. They must have seen me coming because they took off immediately. They headed down the street and ran a stop sign, making a quick right turn.

I jammed on the gas pedal and by the time I got to the stop sign and made the right turn, they were making another right turn through the stop sign on the next block. I knew then that they were running for sure. I hadn't even activated any emergency equipment yet.

As I made the right turn behind them I was closing the gap between us. The car swerved across the center line and nearly ran off of the opposite side of the road. He was still accelerating but I was gaining fast. As I closed the gap to within a few car lengths, I activated my emergency equipment. About that time a long object, looking strangely like a shotgun, came flying out of the vehicle. It crashed onto the pavement in front me and threw out a little burst of sparks as it skipped, flipped and flopped to a stop.

Murphy's law was working quite well as there was so much radio traffic that I had no hope of calling out on my predicament. I knew that the car was fast approaching a major intersection and I just knew there was about to be a horreineous (that's my own word that is a combination of horrible, horrendous, heinous, and hideous) crash. As is often the case with Evil, it blew right through the intersection unscathed. I had to slow down for obvious reasons and as soon as I saw nothing was coming, I punched the accelerator again to make up for lost time.

I knew the road was about to get real curvy and the probability of Evil making it any further was decreasing exponentially with each passing moment. He made it around the first corner but had cut it too closely which made it impossible for him to make the next corner. As we say in driver training, "Early apex equals off-road recovery." He flew off the roadway while spinning wildly. Just as the car stopped, I caught up to it.

Both occupants hit the ground running immediately when, if not before, the car came to rest in the bushes of an office complex. One Evil went south and one Evil went east. I picked the Evil that went east and drove as far as I could before jumping out to confront him on foot. He made it a few yards before his 'perp-luck' ran out. He ran through a hedge that was surrounded by rock walls that were too high to climb.

He chose the only viable escape route which happened to be right through me. He burst out of the bushes headed straight for me. I already had my pistol out because I knew they had one gun and might have another. I tucked my pistol in near to my torso and managed to land a perfectly timed left jab square in Evil's dirty little face. He dropped like a rock. I holstered my weapon and handcuffed him quickly then surveyed the area to make sure that Evil #2 wasn't circling around for an ambush.

The area looked clear so I hoisted Evil up and threw him into my patrol car. I never got the second one but did recover the shotgun and twenty five rounds of ammo, some marijuana and a stolen car that received a surprisingly small amount of damage in the crash. All in all it was a pretty good take compared to what it would have been if I had merely impounded the car the night before.

Both Evils were illegal aliens who made their living stealing. They had been on their way to commit another in a string of armed robberies that they were responsible for in my area.

Good things come to those who wait.

CHAPTER NINE
The Evil Drug Fairy

A curious phenomenon rears its ugly head from time to time. I'm not sure if it's the result of too many fried brain cells from substance abuse, from the preconception that all cops must be morons, or from just plain stupidity on the part of Evil. I have named that phenomenon "The Evil Drug Fairy". Whether you believe in the Evil Drug Fairy or not, she appears way too often to be ignored.

One night, while a couple of other officers and I were conducting what we call "stationary patrol" (that's patrolling without going anywhere, not patrolling the stuff you write letters on) underneath the darkened shelter of a closed gas station island, the peaceful quiet of the post—2:00 AM hour was shattered by the squealing tires of a late model Mitsubishi Montero as it hurriedly sought to vacate from the parking lot of a nearby strip club. ("Strip" in this instance means taking off clothing or getting naked, not long and skinny.) It is not at all out of the ordinary to hear tires squealing out of the parking lot of an establishment where alcohol is one of the main courses but this particular situation was a tad different.

What made it different was the fact that, as the Montero was sliding sideways from the parking lot into the roadway, the driver happened to be firing his .45 caliber semi-auto pistol out of his window in the general direction of the valet parking stand. It took only a moment for our stationary patrol to become considerably more focused and mobile as the three separate vehicles we were operating sprang to life. In no time at all we had closed the gap between us and Evil. We were traveling three cars wide with all of our emergency equipment running as we swooped down on Evil. I fully expected him to run but Evil often surprises us jut as he did this time.

Evil stopped right in the middle of the roadway. Like good little po-lice, it took only a fraction of a second for Evil to be illuminated with more lights than a Hollywood premier night and for us to exit our cars with pistols drawn to confront our prey. The primary officer barked at the driver to put his hands out of the car. Evil complied. We told him to step out of the vehicle but he just kept throwing his hands up screaming one of those all too common bad guy interrogatives, "What are you stoppin' me for?"

Since we, as police, are in the public service industry, and since Evil obviously did not feel the need to come to us, we graciously went to him. We extended him the courtesy of not even having to open his own door as he was extracted from his vehicle through the open driver's window much like a loving father would snatch his precious child from the clutches of a vile kidnapper.

While the primary officer facilitated Evil's close-up inspection of the center-turn-lane asphalt, I dove into the vehicle to locate the weapon. As is so common in such circumstances, from the mouth of Evil came the all too familiar, "Hey you can't look in my car. You're violatin' my rights. That's an illegal search," blah blah blah.

I found the pistol tucked in the pocket in the back of the front passenger seat. Inside the car I could still smell the sweet smell of recently ignited gunpowder. A quick sniff confirmed that the pistol we had found was indeed the likely culprit.

We dispatched another car to check on the valet at the strip club. That unit reported back that the valet was uninjured. The valet told us that he delivered Evil's truck to him, as is the practice with valets. When Evil took possession of the vehicle, he immediately began accusing the valet of "stealing his drugs". It was therefore not a great leap of faith to think that there might be drugs somewhere in Evil's truck. I was pleased that the inside of the truck was fairly clean so searching it would be simple.

The first place I looked was the glove compartment and, lo and behold, there I spied three small plastic baggies. In each of the plastic baggies was a one gram lump of something that looked like dried dog dookey. It smelled like marijuana and tested positive for amphetamines. Apparently it was a composite drug cooked to some anonymous order.

Of course, when confronted with the multiple felony charges and the little baggies of drugs, Evil replied with the stale rhetoric of "Those aren't mine. I don't know what that is." Which brings us to the ubiquitous, yet elusive, Evil Drug Fairy. You see, it happens all the time. An innocent, law abiding, pillar of the community leaves a little cash in some concealed area of his home or automobile and the Evil Drug Fairy comes along and takes the cash and leaves drugs in its place. The fairy always seems to anticipate police presence (she probably has a scanner) and does her dirty deed right before her hapless victim has an unexpected and certainly unwarranted encounter with law enforcement. Then the Evil Drug Fairy sits back and laughs while her target is wrongfully arrested and successfully prosecuted.

I guess I should add that the Evil Drug Fairy is the first cousin of the Evil Pants Fairy. The Evil Drug Fairy and the Evil Pants Fairy seem to regularly work together and may actually be alter egos of the same nefarious entity.

9.2 Crappin' In The Kitchen

I would like to say for the record that I fully support your right to wear whatever clothing you would like (with only minor regulations on things bordering the obscene) but you must also bear in mind that I am fully entitled to make a judgment about you based on the clothing you wear. Ooooh, I used the "j" word. Just like the science of profiling made famous and legitimate by the FBI (one of the things they actually do quite well), most police officers can make relatively accurate assessments of individuals based partly on their appearance. Fair or not it is fact.

We have all seen the "gangsta" clothing that some of today's youth sport so proudly. I am talking about the multiple layers of ultra baggy shirts and baggy pants (for lack of anything better to call them) that ride below the hips held up by a constant hand on the crotch or a super taut belt or rope. This clothing craze was essentially designed by gang bangers. The baggy clothes are used to conceal all manner of weaponry or other contraband used in the gang banger trade. The multiple layers are what the little felony-committing dirtbags use to confuse the police. They commit their crime and/or start fleeing from police while wearing a white jersey (for example) and then run around a corner and dispose of the top layer shirt (or pants) and come out the other side no longer matching the first description given by any possible witnesses.

What I am emphatically **not** saying is that anyone who wears baggy clothes is a criminal. That is simply not true. I am saying that it is one indicator that is common to a certain type of criminal. For that reason alone, you will never see my children dressed that way. How you dress your kids is up to you…and should be.

I highly recommend those types of clothes for criminals and actually wish that the fad would catch on across a broader range of Evil. The reason I like it so much is because not only does it look absolutely hysterical, which makes it a mild form of entertainment, but I have caught several young felony perpetrators that I could not have possibly apprehended were it not for their choice of clothing. They were either trying to hold their pants up and run at the same time, with varying degrees of success, or they got tangled up in that extraneous mass of cloth as they attempted to negotiate some obstacle, like a chain link fence.

Many cases where the gangsta clothes help out the police involve the street corner, drug-dealer type of Evil. The funny thing is that as I was thinking about the different stories I could use in this section, I realized something that made me chuckle. All of the stories I was considering had almost the exact same plot line. So rather than pick any specific ones, I decided to relate that general plot.

Uniformed officers naturally have a handicap when trying to quell this particular type of Evil. We are extremely visible and that makes a surprise attack difficult, but not impossible. Criminals are stupid and lazy; if they weren't they would have jobs. They tend to work in one area and stick to one particular pattern of behavior. They are unique in the animal world in that most creatures, given the choice, will not crap in their own kitchens. This behavior does serve to make their area of operations easy to define. What I have had a measure of success with is a hide in plain sight tactic. Once a problem area was identified, I would just cruise the area in my patrol car as often as possible. Initially, Evil would be noticeably disturbed by my presence and sometimes would even take flight. I would ignore him and simply keep driving.

After a few passes, Evil would become desensitized to my presence, assuming that I would just do those drive-bys indefinitely. That is when I would assemble one or two fellow officers to sneak in on foot. One of us would act as the decoy. The decoy would drive by the suspected drug dealers. They would all watch him to see if he would change his approach that time. That would give the other officers free reign to sneak up on the bad guys. When the decoy reached a distance that in Evil's mind made him no longer a threat, Evil would breathe a sigh of relief and would then get surprised when it was face to face with one of the officers who had snuck up to him on foot.

Sometimes a foot chase erupted but the decoy was in a car and strategically positioned to head them off at the pass. We actually welcome foot chases in those scenarios because flight from the police in and of itself constitutes probable cause for a search and an arrest in most cases (at least under our current state law).

Other times we would employ a tactic that is so simple, officers often overlook it. We would ask, "Do you have any drugs, guns, bombs, needles or anything else that might concern me on or about your person?" Some bad guys actually admit to possessing illegal items right off the bat. They usually say that they were just holding it for someone or something equally ridiculous. Sometimes they try to run away and sometimes they start fighting. The options are numerous and boring.

What is interesting is the vast number of times we get a guy who has some pot or some crack in his pocket and when we confront him with it he responds with, "Where did that come from. That ain't mine."

"Come on now, we found it in your pants pocket."

"These ain't my pants" is a common response along with "That wasn't there a minute ago. I don't know where that came from. You put that there. Blah—blah—blah."

Enter the Evil Pants Fairy; the only other plausible explanation. From there the bad guy's only option is to deploy a countermeasure that is common among criminals and the Democratic Party; "Repeat the lie long enough and hope that it becomes the truth." The only problem with that approach is that, like the Jedi mind trick, it only works on the weak minded.

9.3 Some People Never Learn

One scumbag in particular was hanging out in a "known drug area" and had been there for a substantial amount of time—just loitering. People would come up and talk to him briefly, hand him something and he would hand them something back as surreptitiously as possible. Now to the casual observer, this man's actions would be no more suspicious than your average politician courting voters but to the trained narcotics investigator, it hints of Evil and warrants further investigation.

This situation is ideal for deploying the tactic discussed in the previous section. However, the way that one of our officers chose to approach this situation is a good example of a bad idea, which, for that officer, was to be expected. To give a little background, the officer of whom I am speaking, in the first two years of employment, had the dubious departmental record (as far as I know) of having the most felony perpetrators escape from her custody. Whether it was an unsecured burglar who escaped when she opened the door of her patrol car to yell at him for being Evil, or the assault perpetrator she allowed to walk away in handcuffs never to be seen again, she was notorious for bad tactics. The sad part is that any time we tried to explain to her why her tactics were bad she always had an excuse for why it wasn't her fault and all the blame fell on someone else.

One time after coming back from the firing range and failing to qualify four times in a row on one of the easiest courses in the world, she said that she couldn't shoot because she was under a lot of stress that day. When I added that there is no situation quite as stressful as fighting for your life in a raging gun battle she actually had the gall (I'm not sure if it was unmitigated or not) to say that she could handle that type of stress. What-ever!

Anyway, her method for handling the street corner drug dealer was to walk right up to him (with no backup or other support) with her less than intimidating frame and annoyingly shrill voice and shake her finger directly in his face while telling him that she was going to arrest him. Like so many of his Evil counterparts would have done in a similar situation, Evil gave her a hefty shove, knocked her on her surly (and rather large) behind, and took off running. As was so common for that officer she cried over the radio for some sheepdogs to come and save her.

Within twenty minutes or so we had her bad guy rounded up and safely secured in the back of a patrol car. She wasted no time in repeating her standard operating procedure of opening the door of the patrol car to yell at Evil saying, "You're lucky I'm not the one that caught you."

I remember thinking to myself, "What would you have done...let him knock you on your butt again? Or maybe you would just whine him into submission." Some people never learn.

9.4 They Aren't Real Drugs

There are times when the Evil Drug Fairy is invoked in vain. I was on patrol one night, minding my own business and not bothering anyone when a car on a side street near my location started squealing its tires. I looked and saw the car sliding sideways across the road with no apparent external reason, leading me to believe that it was an intentional and reckless act on the part of the vehicle operator.

Rather than pouncing on him immediately, I watched for a

moment to see his next move. He pulled halfway into a parking lot and stopped. He put the car into reverse and squealed again. He backed out and went into another driveway and stopped. He squealed the tires for the third time and I decided that was a good time for a little face to face encounter.

I maneuvered in behind the car and activated my emergency equipment. The guy pulled over immediately and stopped. There was some movement but nothing that alarmed me excessively. I approached the driver and gave the standard greeting as my flashlight illuminated Evil and my eyes scanned the inside of the car. I made note of several items in the car but saw nothing that constituted cause for immediate concern.

The driver was sweaty and nervous. He apologized about his driving and said he was just screwing around. I went back to my car and watched him intermittently as I wrote out a ticket. I saw him make a movement like he was hiding something under his seat. When I went back to his car, I was giving him my standard ticket spiel when I noticed that one of the items in the car I had made mental note of on our first encounter was no longer there. It was a small felt baggy like the type that Crown Royal bottles come in. It had been located on the center console area and the driver looked as if he was trying to conceal it with his hand the first time.

Evil often gives itself away by making maneuvers or actions that are just strange. Usually those actions are the result of a guilty conscience. Like the maggot who is carrying an illegal weapon who keeps touching it to make sure it's there and still concealed, or the drug user that keeps touching the pocket where his drugs are, this guy was overly protective of an otherwise insignificant little bag. If he was that worried about it, that meant I should be too. I asked him where it was and he gave that all too expected and "reasonable articulable suspicion" inducing answer, "What bag?"

I asked him to step out of the car and detained him while I checked under the seat where I had seen him reach. This may come as a shock to you but there I found the little blue felt bag. Picking it up I could tell that there was something in it that felt suspiciously like pills. Inside I found what later proved to be ecstasy. This particular Evil at first tried to blame the Evil Drug Fairy but when he realized that wasn't going to work, he tried something new.

He said, "I'll be honest with you. I was up at the club selling those to people telling them it was "X" (slang for ecstasy) but they're really just sugar pills. I wouldn't sell real drugs. I'm not like that."

Even if he had been telling the truth, I guess he didn't realize that selling fake drugs is just as illegal as selling the genuine article.

CHAPTER TEN
Why Do You think They Call It Dope?

At the beginning of our shift, another officer and I were dispatched to a call on a signal 25 (shot fired). Just prior to our arrival at the location, our dispatcher deemed it appropriate to advise us that the complainant reported that the signal 25 came from the apartment next door and that the bullet had come through the wall into his apartment.

The other unit and I arrived simultaneously and I approached the door to the caller's apartment first. He saw us coming and greeted us just outside. He said that he had been sitting in his living room watching TV when he heard a loud bang from the apartment directly to our left. He thought he heard a sound in the upstairs area of his own apartment and when he went to look, he found a bullet lying (not laying) on the stairs. He immediately checked on his young son who was sleeping in the upstairs room and finding him okay, he then called 911.

Meanwhile, he watched and waited. He saw someone exit the apartment next door and confronted him briefly. As you might expect, the person denied any knowledge of any gunfire and hurriedly left the scene.

After a cursory inspection of the scene and confirmation that there was indeed a bullet that had entered the complainant's home through the wall from the apartment next door, I naturally decided to knock on the door of the offending apartment.

My backup officer went around behind the apartment in case anyone tried to surreptitiously exit the target location.

To my complete surprise, the door to the apartment opened and I was greeted by a young Indonesian man who had the distinct appearance of someone who was on the downside of a substantial, chemically induced mental vacation.

I asked if anyone else was in the apartment and he said that there was not. He then invited us inside. Naturally my next question referenced the possibility of gunfire originating from his general vicinity. He was certain that he knew nothing about any gunfire and offered to let us look around the apartment.

My partner went upstairs while I remained in the living room with Evil. In no time at all, my partner came back downstairs with a little baggie of white powder and an improvised smoking apparatus. When confronted with the newfound evidence of his misbehavior, the man became curiously nonresponsive.

I asked my partner to sit with Evil for a minute since the initial call was on a gunshot and no gun had been found. I went to check the other upstairs bedroom—the primary reason for that "protective sweep" being, of course, to check for any potential victims or perpetrators. Any evidence left in plain view would just be a bonus.

In the second upstairs bedroom I did not locate any additional perps or victims. What I did happen to stumble across was a soft side suitcase that was partially open. Inside was a large plastic bag and I could see a few oddly colored pills that reminded me of some contraband I had seen once or twice (or a bazillion) times before. Upon further consideration, I thought it prudent to advise my partner that a warrant might be a good idea and that we should secure the premises until we could get one.

The warrant came and we found the gun we had been seeking. It was in a lock box next to the suitcase that had the plastic bag in it. The plastic bag contained the largest single amount of MDMA (commonly known as ecstasy—methylenedioxymethamphetamine) ever recovered in my county and one of the largest in the state up to that point. There were roughly fourteen pounds of pills which equated to about 15,000 hits.

I guess that it really came as no surprise that the Evil we found in the apartment was already on probation for a litany of previous drug charges. Maybe this time he will get deported but I am not holding my breath.

10.2 Have At It

Some people who commented to me on my first book (Searching for Evil and the Perfect Donut—it's really good. You should read it.) seemed a little confused on my stance on controlled substances. I would like to take this opportunity to clarify my position. In a perfect world, I think all people should be free to live as they please as long as in doing so, they do not infringe on the rights of anyone else. In this perfect world, if it were possible for a person to produce and consume whatever manner of substance they wanted to without adversely affecting those around them I would say, "Have at it."

However, this is obviously not a perfect world and I am convinced that the aforementioned scenario is not possible so I tend to lean toward the other extreme. I have been a first hand witness to way too many lives being destroyed by mind altering chemicals. From alcohol to opium and all its derivatives, to methylenedioxywhatchamacallit, and everything in between, we as a society and as individuals suffer enormously because of these substances. Whether it is the drunk driver that damages property and affects insurance rates or even kills someone, the alcoholic who destroys his family and breeds more like himself, the crack addict who steals to support his habit or kills because he's high, or any other number of consequences that we all must suffer, there is no benefit (outside of the limited use of legitimate medicine) to these substances.

Human nature being what it is, I know we will never get rid of them so I suppose that we just have to deal with it. If nothing else, at least I can use it to fill a few pages.

A classic example of a life completely ruined by drugs, specifically cocaine, is found in a man who at one time was the star running back for one of the state universities where I live. He had a promising career ahead of him but instead got addicted to cocaine, dropped out of school, and ended up as one of our regular homeless maggots who is still in and out of prison to this day. The best job he has had since college is as a part time parking lot sweeper at the local gas station.

I will say that ever since our first meeting, our relationship has always been curiously cordial despite the strains placed upon it by multiple felonious perpetrations (on his part of course). I can't remember exactly when it was, but early in my career, he got me confused with another, older officer named Skip. Ever since that time that is what he has called me. I tried correcting him the first few dozen times but it didn't do any good so I just answer to the name now.

Despite the abuse he has subjected himself to over the years, he is still a sizeable fellow. I will freely confess that I am glad as hell he has never tried to fight me because he would absolutely whup my ass. He did make me nervous, though, one night when he was suffering from the effects of some particularly bad drugs.

I had no idea that he was the perpetrator when the call came over the radio of a prowler at an apartment door. Just after dispatching the call, the dispatcher told us that the prowler was trying to force open the door. A few seconds went by before we got another update. The prowler had forced open the door and was inside the apartment.

Two other officers beat me to the scene and called out over the radio that Evil had fled literally seconds before they arrived. To say that he forced open the door was an understatement. He had actually hit it so hard that the entire door frame separated from the building and went crashing into the apartment. Once inside, Evil had ransacked the place while the owner cowered in a corner somewhere praying for the police to hurry up and get there.

The officers at the scene gave his description and last known direction of travel over the radio. One officer stayed to write the report and secure the crime scene while the rest of us went hunting. Only a few minutes passed before an identical call came up in the same apartment complex. Two such violent and conspicuous crimes occurring back to back told us that our bad guy was either really crazy or he was some serious Evil.

I was still in my patrol car circling the area because there were already enough officers out on foot. As the saying goes, you don't want to have all your police officer eggs in one basket. The officers on foot made it to the apartment in time to confront Evil, but somehow Evil got away from them and fled the scene on foot again.

Only a few more minutes passed when I heard, through my open car window, the sound of smashing glass. I drove to the area the sound had come from, which was a dilapidated, single story commercial building that had a convenience store on one end and a dry cleaner/Laundromat on the other. I immediately noticed that the sound of breaking glass had come from the front door of the grocery store, which was in pieces.

I cautiously approached and could hear crashing sounds

coming from inside the store. It sounded as if someone, or something, was tearing the store apart. I didn't have to wait long for a backup officer to show up. We peeked in through the broken front door and, almost immediately, I recognized Evil. Up to that point, I was certain that there was about to be, at the very minimum, a really good fight and possibly even a killin'. Even though I recognized Evil, his behavior was so bizarre that those options were still open.

I called out his name and he froze. He turned to see who it was that was talking to him. Even in his drug induced frenzy he managed to recognize me. It was at that point that he ceased his violence and began pleading for me to help him.

"Skip! You gotta help me man, they're after me."

"Don't worry [Evil] I'll take good care of you. Just come on out."

Still not exactly sure what was going on, I kept my distance as he crept out through the broken door. I directed him over to my car where he calmly submitted to a handcuffing and quietly got into my car. The whole time he just kept muttering, "You gotta protect me Skip. They're after me. You won't let 'em get me Skip. I know you won't." etc. etc. etc.

I breathed a heavy sigh of relief but wasn't completely comfortable until I had deposited him at the county jail with multiple burglary charges and a few incidentals. By then, whatever he was on had begun to wear off and he was more groggy and confused than anything else.

He actually apologized to me the next time I saw him. It wasn't long before he did an encore of that night's performance and ended up with a .357 magnum bullet in his back courtesy of the homeowner whose door he kicked in. After that he went away for quite a while but has since returned to his old haunts. He is getting a little older and who knows, maybe a little wiser.

In the last couple of years at least he has kept a fairly low profile.

10.3 Tick-Tock, Tick-Tock

One of the most entertaining side effects of drug use and abuse is irrational paranoia. Another officer and I were having breakfast at the local IHOP when he got a call to investigate a suspicious noise. The dispatcher paused before letting us know that the suspicious noise was a ticking sound coming from the sink.

I was almost finished with my breakfast and the call sounded fairly entertaining so I asked the other officer to wait for me so that I could go with him. He obliged and a few minutes later we were on our way.

When we got there, the caller was waiting for us outside of his apartment building. Without saying much, he led us up to the apartment and to the offending sink. The primary officer put his ear near the sink and, surprisingly, heard nothing unusual.

The caller said, "Can't you hear it? It's a regular, ticking sound."

The primary officer again listened closely to the sink but it said nothing to him.

"Sorry man. I don't hear anything."

"Huh? Maybe it stopped."

"Is this your medication?"

"Yessir."

"What's it for?"

The caller, smelling faintly of alcohol, declared that it was some antidepressant or antipsychotic or something.

"Are you supposed to drink while you're on this stuff?"

"No sir."

"Have you been?"

"Yessir."

"There's your problem."

The primary officer started for the door. I, however, did not want to let the guy off quite so easily.

"I'm curious as to what you thought the ticking was?"

He tried to avoid the question as he walked us to the door.

"Seriously. You called the police for a reason. What did you think it was."

"Well,... to be honest...I thought it was a bomb."

"Can you think of any reason why someone would want to blow up your sink?"

"No sir."

"Assuming someone did want to blow up your sink, do you have any idea how they would get the bomb down the drain?"

"No sir."

"You see...sometimes if you just take the time to think things through, these little problems just solve themselves."

10.4 Eat It

Drugs not only make people do weird things, they destroy lives. Sometimes they destroy lives over the long haul and sometimes they do it fairly quickly. Whether it's the young basketball star (Len Bias) with the promising professional career right around the corner whose heart explodes with his "first hit" of crack or the nameless scumbag on the side of the road that dies after years of abuse: drugs don't know or care who you are. Drugs are bad. Drugs are Evil. Drugs can ruin your life. Drugs can end your life.

A little episode that reflects a not-so-uncommon occurrence in the law enforcement world involves a particular scumbag who was a petty criminal and just a plain loser. He was a trouble maker—but not too seriously. I guess I could say that he was just a pain in the butt. He happened to frequent a bar where I worked security off duty and was always getting into some kind of minor trouble. That is, until the night when he left that bar with a couple of grams of cocaine in his pocket and got stopped by the police just on the other side of the county line.

They arrested him for DUI and had him in the back of a patrol car in handcuffs. The arresting officer hadn't found the cocaine in his pocket and to avoid that additional felony charge, Evil thought it would be a good idea to try to eat it. He maneuvered the cuffs around to where he could reach the contraband and sure enough he got it into his mouth.

By the time the officer finished his on-scene paperwork, Evil was dead. Tragic, isn't it?

10.5 The Hookers Must Have Left Them There

There is a hotel across the street from one of our strip clubs that, not surprisingly, is a welcome refuge for guys who pick up girls or just hire them at the club for a "private performance". I know it is really hard to believe that there are drugs and prostitution in strip clubs but it really does happen…occasionally.

Security at this hotel was doing rounds on each of the floors when he came across an unusual sight. He found a naked man with only one leg unconscious in the hallway. The missing leg was not a recent development; it was one he had obviously lived with for a while.

The security guard called 911 and before long I was on the way. When I got there, the security guard led me to the floor in question and sure enough, the guy was still there. He started to regain a little consciousness and had no clue where he was or why. I asked security if he was a guest and they said that he was.

They pointed out his room, which happened to be fairly near to where he was lying (not laying).

When I went to his room I found that the door had been left slightly ajar. Still not certain what had transpired, I thought it might be a good idea to perform a cursory check of the room to check for possible additional victims or perpetrators. When I walked into the hotel room I found neither. What I did find was a large bag of a white powdery substance in plain view on the bed. Call me cynical but my first notion was that the bag might contain contraband. Chemical tests later proved my initial assumption to be correct. It was cocaine…lots of cocaine.

When confronted with this development after he had regained consciousness, Evil said, "Those drugs aren't mine. I have no idea where they came from. The hookers must have left them there." I guess he hadn't heard about the Evil Drug Fairy.

Don't worry, the judge didn't buy it either.

10.6 Dude, The Cops Are On The Way

One of the funny things about people who are under the influence of mind-altering chemicals is how easy they are to mess with. I was on my way to a medium priority call when just before turning off of the main road, I saw a curious sight on the roadway in front of me. There is a big bridge that serves as a jurisdictional boundary between my county and an adjacent city. In the middle of the bridge is a median that is about ten or twelve inches high and three feet wide. That makes it just large enough for people who aren't paying attention to drive up on top of it and get stuck.

What I saw on the bridge was a pickup truck that had made it at least half way across the bridge before finally bottoming out on the median. I had seen vehicles get stuck on the median before but had never seen one make it that far. I decided to take a little detour from my dispatched call to go see how he had gotten stuck so far out. I pulled up next to him and our driver's sides were opposite each other so that we could speak through our open windows without having to get out of our cars.

The driver of the other vehicle looked like he was hammered (technical term for intoxicated). Even while sitting down he was swaying back and forth with both his eyes and his mouth wide open. He was messing with his gear shift and didn't even notice that I had pulled up. Once he had gotten the car into 'drive' he mashed on the gas pedal. The car was just far enough off of the pavement so that the tires were still touching but there wasn't enough friction to move the car forward over the concrete median. Consequently, the tires started squealing and smoking but the car wouldn't move.

The driver had this amazing, puzzled look on his face. He stopped what he was doing and glanced in my direction. He was obviously surprised to see me and looked to be at a loss for words.

I said, "Hey man, what's goin' on?"

"There's somethin' wrong with my car."

"Well, I tell ya bud; your car's bottomed out on the median. I think you're goin' to need a tow truck."

With that, he leaned out of his open window and looked groundward.

"Whoa! How'd that get there?"

I had to get to my other call so I figured I would take a second to screw with him. It was obvious that his car wasn't going anywhere so any immediate threat that his condition posed was not serious.

I said, "Lemme tell ya somethin' bud. If I were you I would turn the car off and get into the passenger seat before the cops get here. If they catch you in the driver seat, especially with the motor runnin', they're likely to take your ass to jail."

"I don't wanna go to jail," he slurred.

"Well skooch on over then. The cops are on the way."

With that I took off in my marked patrol car and headed for my original call. About that time radio dispatched another car to a call on a vehicle stuck on the median on the bridge. I gave a little chuckle and continued on to my call.

After I handled my call I went back to the bridge. The other officer had pulled up and found the guy in much the same condition as I had. Evil was now handcuffed in the back of the other officer's car, under arrest for D.U.I. I asked the officer what had happened and he told me that he had pulled up and Evil was in the driver's seat trying to drive the car off of the median.

In the immortal words of Bugs Bunny, "What a maroon."

10.7 Sniff This

It never ceases to amaze me what people will do to get high. They will drink shoe polish filtered through stale bread, they will smoke anything they can fit into a pipe, they will overdose on all manner of over the counter chemicals just to see which ones make them feel good, they will sniff glue or spray paint up their noses or inhale butane from their cigarette lighter refills. There is really no end to what people will try in the name of getting high. (Hey, that rhymes.)

I thought that inhalants were something limited to high school kids until one night when I responded to a motor vehicle accident. There was a woman in her late twenties or early thirties who apparently had an addiction to sniffing those little propellant canisters that have all different types of innocuous applications like dispensing whipped cream or decorative cake icing.

She was doing her sniffing while she was driving and apparently was so preoccupied that, even though it was near midnight and she was traveling on an unlighted interstate highway, she forgot to turn on her headlights. An unfortunate side effect of not having illumination on the roadway in front of her was that she either didn't see that exit ramp—or if she saw the ramp, she didn't see the concrete wall across the far side of the intersection at the bottom of the ramp. She hit the wall running at least 60 mph and by all accounts was probably dead on impact.

An interesting thing about the accident was that when we examined the brake light filaments, they indicated that at the time of impact, she did not have her foot on the brake.

All I could think was, "That must have been a big, all be it short lived, surprise."

10.8 On The Boardwalk

I really didn't intend to have so many stories about intoxicated drivers, but they are just so darn prevalent and generally entertaining that it just sort of worked out that way.

We often get calls from citizens in reference to possible intoxicated drivers. Sometimes they pan out and sometimes they don't. We try to investigate them all nonetheless. One such call originated from a resident of an apartment complex who wanted the police to come to investigate a possible drunk driver in the parking lot. (Driving under the influence is one of the few traffic related crimes that we can arrest someone for on private property. Most other traffic laws only apply to public roadways.) I went out to the scene and didn't locate anything, so I left.

The resident called back shortly thereafter and was all mad because I didn't do anything about the drunk driver. I returned to the scene and discovered that one vital bit of information had been excluded from my initial dispatch.

The car wasn't in the parking lot near the building, it had driven around the back side of the building through the woods, onto a landscaped walking path, and then onto a boardwalk of sorts that led out to a gazebo that overlooked a manmade lake. Luckily for the coked up driver, the boardwalk narrowed progressively toward the gazebo to the point where the car was too wide to proceed. The right front wheel caught on a support pillar and was sheered off of the car. The driver managed to make the vehicle limp another couple of feet to where it got so tightly wedged between the railings that the tow truck nearly tore up the whole boardwalk trying to extricate it.

When I asked the driver, who was still trying to drive the stuck and wheel-less car, what the hell he was doing, he said, "I just wanted to park closer to my apartment."

10.9 Dumb and Dumberer

When I get into "ticket-writin'" mode, I occasionally take up a position on an Interstate highway entrance ramp and watch for cars to zoom by at speeds that are obviously a bit above the posted maximum. Anyone who has ever driven the highways of Atlanta knows that drivers here seem to think that speed limits are merely a suggestion. I'll admit that part of the responsibility for that condition lies with the enforcement officers. I, like so many other officers in the area, rarely even think of stopping a car unless it is doing in excess of 20 mph over the posted limit. It's not because we are lazy, it's just because there are so many people going so fast that we like to pick the cream of the crop. It is not at all uncommon to find vehicles traveling in excess of 100 mph and for some reason it seems that the heavier traffic is, the faster everyone tries to go.

One afternoon in the pre-rush-hour traffic, I was strategically positioned at the top of an entrance ramp that was one exit away from my jurisdiction. (The reason for that was so that by the time I caught up to my quarry, I would just be crossing into my jurisdiction and that would give me more time to orchestrate the traffic stop.) Like any good police officer, I had my window down so I could hear what was going on around me. The steady, dull drone of the highway traffic was gradually interrupted by the unmistakable bleat of a speeding motorcycle. The ultra-high pitch of the whining motor told me that it must be going fast—really fast.

Before I even saw the bike, I stomped on my accelerator with every ounce of energy I had, as if the harder I pushed on it the faster my car would go. The rapid crescendo of the approaching engine peaked as not one, but two 'rice-burning' 'crotch rockets' blew by me at roughly mach 5 before I had even made it half way down the entrance ramp. Though I was relatively certain that it was an exercise in futility, I kept up my pitiful but valiant attempt to catch up to the bikes, thinking that I would at least go one or two exits into my jurisdiction before admitting defeat.

Just as I rounded a broad curve in the Interstate, I saw brake lights, smoke and some erratic driving on the part of a couple of cars just within my field of view. My first thought was that both of the bikes had wrecked and I was about to witness poetic justice first hand. I started slowing down so I could survey the scene as I approached without becoming part of it. There was one car that had apparently careened off to the left and had collided with the median wall and another car. There was a whole lot of debris in the roadway and nice, fresh, black skid marks that seemed to go haphazardly all across the roadway. I could see what looked like the remains of a motorcycle off to the right side of the road and at that point, people were just starting to exit their cars to try to offer aid or just to gawk at the carnage that spilled out before them.

Much to my surprise, the motorcyclist was alive. He had a broken leg and was taking his injury rather well. His lack of reaction to the excruciating pain of a compound fracture to the femur was likely due to his recent ingestion of cocaine; the remnants of which I found in a plastic baggie in the storage compartment on his bike. He was coherent enough to tell me that he was just driving down the road when somebody changed lanes in front of him and they crashed. He conveniently neglected to mention that he was running about 120 mph at the time. Since he didn't know I had been trying to catch up to him, I thought I would just ask if he was riding with anyone. He said that he and his buddy were going to a bar that was just off of the next exit.

I turned him over to the paramedics and continued with the crash investigation and report. Just as I was wrapping things up, my last order of business was to run an NCIC check of the motorcycle. Besides the plethora of traffic charges and the cocaine possession charge, Evil was also going to get a 'Theft By Receiving Stolen Motorcycle' charge. It was then that I decided that it might be prudent to go to that bar and try to locate his friend. At the very least I would get another traffic ticket or two and, hopefully, I would get something more.

As I pulled into the parking lot, there was one little motorcycle parked right by the front door. I asked the doorman where the driver was and he pointed the guy out to me. I asked the man to accompany me outside and he did. I asked if that was his bike and he reluctantly said that it was. I then asked him if he knew the guy that had been in the wreck and he said that he did. I continued with my interrogation that was ingeniously contrived to get Evil to incriminate himself and when I was confident that I could make at least a traffic case, I secured him in my patrol car. About that time, my dispatcher came back with the delayed response on the NCIC check I had run on his license plate. Surprise, surprise, surprise; it was stolen too. A search of his person incident to arrest produced his small stash of cocaine also.

If all bad guys were that stupid, crime fighting would be a breeze.

10.10 The Internet Made Me Do It

There are addictions that can cause symptoms much like those of substance abuse but have no connection whatsoever to chemical substances. A case-in-point is the following story.

I was just coming out of the precinct on my way to my beat when I noticed an Asian man and woman who looked particularly distraught and confused, standing in the parking lot. They looked as if they desperately wanted to ask someone a question but were afraid to approach any of the uniformed personnel who were purposefully walking to and from the building, either preoccupied with going to work or glad to be going home.

I made it a point to approach them with a friendly smile and ask them if they needed some assistance. They looked relieved and almost immediately began spilling out their problems to me. They explained to me that their teenage son was in his final year of high school when, because of the father's business, they had to relocate from one of the northern states down to the area around our police station. Before they moved, their son had been a star basketball player and straight-A student. He was popular in school and had lots of friends. By all appearances he was a well adjusted young man with a bright and promising future.

All that changed when they moved. Almost immediately their son became despondent and his grades started dropping. He didn't even try to make new friends and lost contact with his old ones. He quit basketball and withdrew to the quiet refuge of his room and his computer. He became literally obsessed with surfing the internet and seemed to be spending more and more time with his computer and away from peers, family and school.

They were worried about him and didn't know what they should do.

I tried to be understanding and patient but also had to explain to them that their problem really wasn't a police matter and that they needed to find a counselor or a psychiatric professional to help them with their problem. Though I did nothing for them and I could see it in their eyes, they thanked me quite sincerely and left.

A month or three went by and my encounter with the reticent couple had been all but forgotten. I got a call on a domestic disturbance in one of the middle class neighborhoods near our precinct. I had a trainee with me and no other backup was available. I hoped that we wouldn't need it and we proceeded to the call. When we pulled up in the cul de sac near the target address, we were met by a man and woman. I didn't recognize them at first but they recognized me. It took a minute for them to remind me who they were but after that we were like old friends. They told me that their son had gotten worse since we had spoken last and that earlier in the day, the situation began spiraling furiously downward.

It seems that due to fate, satanic influence, sun spots or whatever else you want to blame bad things on, the family's primary internet provider had gone down. The son's obsession with the internet had reached monumental proportions. When the service provider went down, he naturally thought that Mom and Dad were responsible. That was the straw that snapped the kid's fragile mind. After that there was a heated argument. They started to explain what he did in his blind rage but cut themselves off saying that I should just go take a look for myself and everything would be clear.

I led my trainee around the side of the house to the primary entrance which led us into the kitchen. Through a small window

I caught a glimpse of the carnage that required police presence but didn't really begin to appreciate it until I went inside. The kitchen was destroyed. There was a small fire burning in the microwave. Splintered furniture littered the floor and food was strewn all over everything that I could see. There were broken eggs and rice smeared on the wall and who knows what else was in the mix. It looked as if everything that could have been emptied, broken, turned over or smashed—was.

I turned to see if the couple had followed me into the house and they had. I asked which way was the quickest way to the boy's room. They told me that it was at the top of the stairs that were just outside the kitchen and down the hall. I told them to wait there and suggested that they put out the fire in the microwave while I was gone.

With trainee in tow, I crept through the house, up the stairs and stopped just before the doorway that I knew had to be the boy's room. There was the eerie glow associated with the cathode ray tube of a TV or computer monitor casting oblong shadows into the hall. No other light was available. I peeked into the room and saw the only undisturbed item in the whole house. There sat the boy in front of his computer table, staring at the blank screen that undoubtedly flashed some mundane error message. Who knows what it was saying to him. He was gently rocking back and forth and seemed to be on his own plane of reality.

I signaled for my trainee to cover me while I made entry to the room and took up a position of advantage in case things turned ugly. I knew that he had to know that I was there but he made no acknowledgement. I broke the tense silence with a typical, "What's goin' on?"

"Nothin'," he replied very matter-of-fact-ly.

"Well it looks like somethin' happened. Why don't you tell me about it?"

"I just got a little mad. That's all. I'm fine now."

He still hadn't looked at me and if it weren't for the fact that I knew he was the one talking, I still would have had no evidence that he was even remotely in touch with the real world. I spoke to him a little and explained that he would have to go see somebody to work through his "problem". He was very quiet and submissive and allowed us to handcuff him without offering any resistance. We walked him to the patrol car in order to transport him to the juvenile mental treatment facility (nut house or looney bin for short).

Just as we were backing out of the driveway, we saw a sight that can send chills up the spine of even the most seasoned of officers—the sight of a supervisor arriving at the scene. He made it a point to park in such a manner that I could not leave and would have to get out of my car to talk to him.

He asked me what was going on and I, being a believer in the axiom that the less you say—the less trouble you are likely to get in, said something to the effect of, "The kid went crazy and needs to go to the hospital so we are taking him."

I should have known that would not be enough to placate the boss. He said that he needed to go see what had happened since he heard that the call was dispatched as a fight. I tried to show him all the damage and explain the crazy behavior (including the history) as quickly as possible, hoping we would be able to get on with our transport. That would not be the case. In his infinite, supervisory wisdom, he surveyed the scene and declared magnanimously that the young man was obviously a criminal and needed to be arrested and taken to jail rather than taken for psychiatric help.

I couldn't believe my ears and tried to plead my case with

him. I pointed out that for there to be a crime, the person committing it has to have intent. If he's crazy then it's not really a crime (at least in this type of case). As you might guess, he was un-swayed in his decision. Not being one to provoke a physical fight with someone who outranks me and realizing that my temper was fast reaching the point where such a confrontation would be unavoidable, I got back into the car with my trainee and crazy boy. I took a deep breath and looked at my trainee and said, "Don't ever do what I am about to do."

Sorry. I didn't do anything destructive or violent in the physical sense. I picked up the cell phone and called the boss' boss. I explained to him in vivid detail the circumstances surrounding our call. I intentionally did not tell him what my immediate supervisor had directed me to do.

He responded with, "You're going to take him to the mental hospital, right?"

I said, "Yes sir. If you say so sir," and off we went.

My boss didn't realize what had transpired until after we were on the way back from the hospital. Needless to say, he was pissed. When I walked into the precinct he was having one of those closed door meetings with his boss. There was lots of yelling and stuff but when the door opened, everyone feigned a calm civility. My boss instructed me to write a criminal report on damage to property listing the boy as the offender but stating that he was transported to the hospital rather than being arrested.

It never ceases to amaze me how grown men can act like little children, especially in the government.

10.11 Heaven

This last story is one that to me was a bit disturbing. Anyone who knows me knows that when bad things happen to kids, it bothers me. Kids in this day and age have enough problems to deal with, I think, without compounding them by adding dangerous drugs to the mix. Unfortunately, many times whatever it is that they are looking for, they can't find at home or amongst their friends and often they turn to drugs.

This little girl probably wasn't any more than 16 years old but she had already moved out of her family's home and into a small rented house with some of her friends. They weren't really bad kids, I guess, but they did drink a little too much and they liked to smoke pot. She had just finished doing at least those two things and maybe more when she told her friends that she was going outside in the post midnight air to take a walk. They didn't pay much attention as she staggered out the front door.

An hour or so passed before the friends started to get worried that she had not returned. One of them finally decided to go look for her. He didn't have to go far to find her. About fifteen feet from the front door there was a large oak tree. This was one of those trees that had been growing for over 100 years I am sure and maybe over 200. It was massive. If there had been any druids around they probably would have been worshipping it. The Keebler elves could've opened a satellite factory in this tree. I'm talking big.

But anyway, that tree must have held some sort of attraction for that confused little girl because she chose it as the instrument of her death. She was found hanging by her neck from a rope that was attached to one of the lower limbs. Her pale, fragile little body was dangling mere inches from the solid ground that would have given her a second chance. Her face looked like a china doll. Her eyes were still open and eerily peaceful. Her final gaze fixed upon some unknown, distant vision.

I remember that the night was unusually still and to add to that very disturbing scene was one thing I don't think that I will ever forget. She was wearing a faded pink shirt with the word "HEAVEN" written across the front. What a terrible waste.

CHAPTER ELEVEN
Super Evil

Super Evil is a term I like to give to those criminals who seem to be able to accomplish superhuman feats during the course of their attempted escape from law enforcement. Their abilities may be augmented because of the ingestion of some controlled substance, the presence of abnormally high amounts of adrenaline or just by seemingly demonic possession. These forces can also work in combination with one another to cause individuals to do some very impressive things.

Early one morning I was driving down the road in a security truck that I operate one night a week to help make ends meet. I happened to be approaching one of our local strip clubs when I saw a young man run across the street in front of me. He was wearing camouflage pants and no shirt. Since the strip club in question was an all female club, there was no reason for any half naked men to be anywhere close by and especially not in public. Since it looked a bit curious to me, I pulled my truck into an adjacent parking lot to see if I could discern what was happening.

I drove completely around the building where I thought the potential Evil had run but could not locate him. I decided to sit in the parking lot to see if he materialized. I didn't have to wait long before I heard the sound of a young man screaming. It was garbled at first but as I rolled down my window and listened, I could tell that he was screaming obscenities.

The noise stopped. I looked around to see where it had come from, but again saw nothing. Then it started again. This reminds me of something I forgot to mention in the tracking chapter. Try to remember to think in three dimensions rather than two. Sometimes all you need to do to find Evil is to look up.

"Fuck all you mother fuckers god dammit. I'm gonna kick your asses," I heard the voice say from its still unknown location.

I knew by the volume that he had to be close and couldn't believe that I had not seen him yet. Then the corner of my eye picked up some movement on the roof of the liquor store that was a little less than a block away. I saw what looked like the same figure that had run across the road earlier. He stood up on the roof just enough to see over the sign on the front of the building and continued his verbal assault. I laughed right away because I couldn't help but remember a scene from Monty Python's Holy Grail where the French knights were on the top of the castle taunting King Arthur and his Men. Though I half expected it, he made no reference to "filthy English kaniggits" or to "wipers of other people's bottoms".

Before I could quit laughing, he must have jumped up, then yelled some more insults, crouched down and jumped back up again at least three more times. I had just passed the beat car at a drug store about a quarter of a mile away. I have a rule about getting on the radio when I'm off duty: I don't do it unless it's an extreme emergency. This wasn't. So, I called the beat car on my cell phone and told him that if he wanted some entertainment, he could come try to get the drunk guy off the roof of the liquor store.

He was up for some amusement so he came to my location. By then, the taunting Evil may have seen us because he was staying hidden behind the sign on the roof. The beat officer and I started trying to figure out how to get up on the roof. I've been back to that location several times since and still have no idea how he managed to climb onto the roof. The only explanation that seems to fit is that he was part Tigger: you know—"top made out of rubber, bottom made out of springs." Anyway, my plan was to park my truck next to the building and use it as a ladder. In the meantime, I asked the beat car to go around to the front and distract him somehow.

I was almost in place when the beat officer got around to the front of the building and challenged Evil. It was then that Evil ran across the roof in a direction that put him halfway between me and the other officer. He took a flying leap off of the roof and onto the pavement below. He landed on his feet and barely paused before running away. The beat officer was in hot pursuit on foot so I opted to jump into my truck.

I circled around the building in the direction that the officer and perpetrator had gone. I caught sight of the officer chasing Evil around the side of another building one street over. I drove around the building to cut him off. When he saw me coming, he circled back around the building to his right and headed back toward the other officer.

I continued my circle around to the opposite side only to see the officer rejoin the pursuit. The officer chased Evil up to a driveway that led to near where I was. One side of that driveway had a large stone wall and the other was thick with Holly bushes. I headed for the end of the driveway to cut Evil off, once and for all.

I'll never forget the look on his face when he saw my truck barreling toward him. He was back-stepping and ran right into the wall. It was then that I realized that my security truck's brakes weren't working so well. I thought for a second that I was going to squish him between the truck and the wall and wondered just how I was going to explain that one. While my career flashed before me, the truck whined and groaned to a stop.

Evil was stunned and paused long enough for me to get out of the truck. I ran around behind my vehicle since I didn't think I had room to go around the driver side. Before I could get to Evil, however, he recovered from his moment of shock and ran straight toward the front passenger door of my security truck. Much to my surprise and dismay, he jumped right into the truck. Now it was no longer my entire career flashing before my eyes but merely my well paying and steady extra job. Not quite as bad, but still bad.

Luckily, Evil did not have the presence of mind to lock the door. I was able to climb into my truck just as he was skooching into the driver's seat.

Since he had no shirt on, I grabbed the next best thing—his hair. Where the head goes, the body follows. In this case it was right out the door he had climbed in. Instead of landing on his feet, this time he landed on his face thanks to a strategically timed release on my part.

Then it was time for a precisely executed, top secret police maneuver known as the dog-pile. Evil put up a valiant fight, all the while screaming, "I ain't got no problem with ya'll. Ya'll are my brothers. Ya'll are my people..." I never did figure out exactly what he was talking about. Not wanting to press my luck any further, I chose to leave at that point.

II.2 There Can Be Only One

When the first officer arrived at the scene of a local deli moments after receiving the alarm call, he found a mound of shattered glass that was all that remained of the back door. The business was fairly large and occupied an end suite in a strip shopping center. ("Strip" in this instance means long and skinny, not taking off clothing or getting naked.) As the officer surveyed the scene he looked into the business. At the opposite side of the restaurant he could see another smashed out door. Looking through the business, his eye then caught some movement in the distance. As he concentrated on that movement he could tell it was the figure of a man scurrying across the roof of the department store next door.

He radioed his situation to responding units as he closed the distance between himself and suspected Evil. By the time he got to the department store building, the figure he had seen was no longer visible. By then, several more police units had arrived and were briefed on the situation. They made the collective decision to have a fire truck respond with a ladder tall enough to reach the roof of the building which was approximately twenty-five feet high.

The ladder truck was quick to respond and in no time at all, three officers made their way onto the roof while one or two others remained at ground level. When they first looked around, they spotted a man sitting on the back side of the building dangling his feet over the edge, seemingly oblivious to his surroundings. One officer approached and challenged the man. The man snapped to his feet and looked like he was ready to fight.

The officer whipped open his expandable baton and moved on Evil's position. Evil picked up a PVC pipe that was nearby and prepared to duel with the approaching officer. According to one of the guys on the roof at the time, what happened next was comical. The two men engaged each other in somewhat of a mock swordfight with the officer striking at Evil with the baton and Evil blocking the officer's blows with his PVC pipe. The only thing that would have made it more amusing would have been if Freddy Mercury was singing in the background as someone yelled out, "There can be only one." (This refers to the movie "Highlander", starring Christopher Lambert and featuring music from "Queen".)

After a few blows had been exchanged, Evil decided that it was a good time to take flight. He ran along the back wall of the roof while the three officers closed in. As he neared the end of the roof, the officers knew they had him cornered and were prepared for a fight. Evil robbed them of their capture by taking a flying leap off of the roof onto the asphalt some 25 feet below; a feat that would have likely maimed or killed an ordinary mortal.

There was an officer on the ground near where Evil landed. He said that when the body came plummeting to terra-firma, it landed on its feet, collapsed to its butt and then jumped up and ran off. The officer was stunned by what he had seen but was able to give chase across the parking lot to a chain link fence. Evil easily leapt over the fence with perpetrator ease and the officer thought he could too. The fence was just a little higher than expected and the next thing you know, the good guy's crotch was snagged on top of the fence, allowing for Evil to gain a sizeable lead while the officer tried to prevent a spontaneous vasectomy.

Evil wasted no time in his escape and ran straight toward an adjacent apartment complex. Once he arrived at the closest building, Evil started climbing. He jumped onto the rail of a first floor deck and muscled his way up to a second floor balcony. He repeated the tactic and landed on a third floor balcony where he found an exercise bike that he promptly hoisted over his head and tossed through a plate glass door.

Of course the door shattered instantly and Evil ran inside the apartment. The Mexican family inside was startled awake by the breaking glass and went to see what had happened. They didn't speak much English but Evil was somehow able to communicate to them that he was being chased. However, he told the residents that it was a gang trying to kill him and that he needed their help.

By the time officers swarmed the floor of the building where Evil was holed up, Evil had the entire family braced up against the door to prevent anyone from coming inside. The poor Mexican family must have been scared to death as the alleged "gang" began trying to break in the front door to their apartment.

About that time, Evil decided to poke his head out into the hallway through an alternate door that lead from the kitchen to the hallway. One of the officers noticed him and shouted, "He's over there!"

All of the officers moved from the front door to the kitchen door while Evil simultaneously ran and got the Mexican family to move their body barricade to the kitchen door. While the officers were hammering on the second door, one officer stayed behind at the first door. He calmly turned the handle and surprise, the door opened.

He crept into the apartment and could hear Evil frantically instructing the bewildered Mexicans to hold the kitchen door. The officer grabbed Evil from behind and the fight was on. Thankfully, the Mexican family all recognized the police uniform and quit holding the door. All of the officers left in the hallway then, like water through a collapsing dam, spilled into the crowded kitchen.

The first officer was still striking Evil when the supervisor walked in.

"Uhhh. I think you need to stop hitting him now," the supervisor directed in a less than commanding tone.

"He's got my dick!" the officer yelled back in an abnormally shrill tone as he continued to pound on Evil. After taking a beating that would have laid out any normal man, Evil finally released the officer's private parts and was taken into custody.

Evil later told the judge that he had no recollection of that night's events and suspected that while he was at a local bar, his drink was spiked with something that caused his aberrant behavior. I don't think he ever apologized for the "dick thing" though.

CHAPTER TWELVE
Splattus Maximus

Most suicide calls where the person hasn't actually done the deed raise the question of commitment. It has been my experience that the vast majority of times if the person threatening to commit suicide hasn't done it by the time you get there, they really don't want to. They either want attention or they want you to talk them out of it. The third possibility of course is that they want you to do it for them. Whatever the reason, someone bent on killing themselves will usually create an environment where there will be no one to interfere.

If I were going to take my own life, I would probably pick something that would be quick and relatively painless. Suffocating with carbon monoxide wouldn't be so bad except for the fact that someone might save you right after you have sustained enough brain damage to survive as a vegetable for years to come.

Pills might not be so bad either except for the same problem. They take too long and there's always the chance that someone might rescue you just in time for you to suffer hideous medical side effects from your overdose. (I see a lot of young people who try to get attention by overdosing on acetaminophen. Most of them don't know that it is almost impossible to kill yourself that way but you are almost guaranteed to have irreversible liver damage.)

There's death by fire which to me would be one of the worst. Way too much pain involved. Death by drowning would be pretty crappy too because it just doesn't seem to happen quickly enough. Suffocation poses the same problem and come to think of it, so does hanging.

Then there's jumping off of something really high onto something really hard. Again, there's way too much time from inception to completion to reconsider or regret your choice. Massive deceleration trauma just looks so darn painful that I definitely wouldn't pick that one. Plus, it is usually very messy, and it's rude not to clean up your after yourself. There is always the chance that you might not pick an object high enough or a landing point hard enough and instead of dying on impact, you suffer for a literal lifetime.

Gunshots can be pretty effective but they aren't foolproof and once again you have that problem of all the mess that's left behind.

There is the classic slitting of wrists but, oh my goodness, what a painful thing to do to yourself. Most of the time, people don't hit the right artery and they don't die. Either way, it's too much pain and not enough certainty.

The only method left I can think of is training for years as a Buddhist monk and learning how to meditate yourself to death. I just don't think I have enough commitment for that either.

How about that! I just talked myself out of suicide. I think if I ever had the urge to kill myself though, I would first try bungee jumping. As the saying goes, it's suicide without the commitment. I guess you could say it is sort of like practice suicide. You get all the feeling of dying without the *splattus maximus*.

In the first Searching for Evil book, I devoted an entire chapter to suicides and many of the aforementioned methods were covered in detail. In this book, I am just going to hit the highlights. The term "Splattus Maximus" is Coyote Latin.

Hopefully, no explanation of its cartoon origins is required. I hope that it adequately sets the tone for the following passages.

One suicide that for some reason has cemented itself in my memory started, as many such calls do, with a friend or relative calling the police to check on the subject whom they have not heard from in a while or who was exhibiting "strange behavior". That was the case on one particular evening when a young lady asked us to check on her friend.

The friend was recently divorced and had been despondent for a while blah blah blah. Same song—different verse. We headed for the address in question and were met at the foot of the abnormally long driveway by the woman who had called in the complaint. We asked her to wait by the street while we went to check things out. It's never good to be there with the loved one when the rotting, dead, maggot-infested body is located.

We decided to walk up the driveway unannounced because any time that there is a possibility of encountering a suicidal person, you have to approach as you would any known wanted felon because suicidal people (oddly enough) sometimes do strange things. It is not uncommon for someone to commit "suicide by police". If you recall, we discussed the concept in Chapter One.

Anyway, we crept up the driveway and as soon as I saw into the garage, I got a sneaking suspicion that the complainant's suspicions were correct. It doesn't take a seasoned detective or super sleuth to realize that when there's enough blood on the floor of a room for it to puddle up and start seeping through the ceiling and dripping onto the floor of the room below (in this case the garage) that the person from whom the juice was flowing is not likely to be able to survive.

The complainant had been kind enough to provide us with a key so we went inside to confirm what we all already knew.

In the home/office that was above the garage, our despondent divorcee had chosen as her means of departure a well placed egg mcmagnum—sunny side up. For those of you who are in need of an explanation, she stuck the barrel of a .357 magnum revolver in her mouth and pulled the trigger. Now think back to the old TV commercial... "This is your brain. This is your brain on drugs." This is your brain on a high velocity projectile. Any questions? Apparently the bullet did not immediately kill her because her heart pumped long enough to get all that blood out.

12.2 Happy Leap Year

Sometimes even the most morbid scenes have their own unique bit of humor providing, of course, that you can stay detached. To illustrate what I'm talking about, I'll take you back to an incident that happened at one of those mid-priced hotels that caters to business people.

There was a businessman, a stockbroker I believe, who had been staying in this hotel for a few months. He had divorced his wife and was content to live in the hotel. Perhaps his relationship with his wife had diminished into something that could be paralleled by the services offered at your average hotel. Nevertheless, by all accounts he seemed happy there.

He had also found a much younger woman with whom he could start a relationship. The man's family was aware of her and was not particularly thrilled by her.

On the day of his daughter's high school graduation, the man had planned a dinner date with his significant other and somehow or another the entire family ended up at the same place. One thing led to another and a fairly large verbal altercation erupted in the restaurant. The end result of that altercation was the man's daughter had some choice words for him that ended in "Fuck you, Dad," and the girlfriend left in tears telling him that he needed to go fix his family's problems before coming back to her.

He went back to his hotel/home and sulked and pouted and did whatever it is that people do right before they kill themselves. At some point, the man had a rather cryptic conversation with his son over the phone that prompted the son to become concerned and to go seek out his dad at the hotel. Due to company policy, the hotel clerk wouldn't let the son know what room his dad was in. Meanwhile, dad had rented a second room on the top floor of the hotel under the guise that it was for a visiting friend.

The son went 'round and 'round with the hotel clerk over the release of the room number and when he determined that he was at an impasse, he called the police. We showed up and got the story from the son. The hotel clerk agreed to let us have the room numbers so we could go check on him. We decided to go to the room he had rented on the fourth floor first and if he wasn't there, we would head for the seventh floor room, which was the one he had rented last.

Knowing that we were checking the first room, the son proceeded up to the other room without us. Just as we had determined that there was no one in the first room, I heard the son screaming as he ran down the stairs in the stairwell right next to where we were, "Get some help, he jumped out the window!"

While making my way down the stairs, I called for the paramedics who were staging nearby to head for the rear of the hotel. The bottom of the stairs fed out into the rear parking lot. As a result of the security conscious world with which we have burdened ourselves, the door to the stairs was designed to lock behind us. The entire hotel compound was, unbeknownst to me, only accessible via the front entrance. The front entrance was the point farthest away from where we were.

The exit door from the stairwell put me right next to the pool area and the ten foot tall wrought iron fence that kept all sort of things out, including me. The dilemma was that not one foot from the fence, on the opposite side, was where the man had landed after his seven story swan dive. The frantic son had found his way into the pool enclosure and was obviously distraught. There was a pedestrian gate near my location that was 'exit only' and I couldn't get the son to let me in. The next thing I knew, there was a strange, blonde female who casually walked up to the body and looked at it queerly.

"Is he dead?" she asked to no one in particular.

She looked like she too was on another planet but I still tried to get her attention to coax her into opening the gate so we could come in without having to go around. She walked around in circles for a minute and then disappeared into the inside of the hotel. By this time, the paramedics had arrived on my side of the fence and we still couldn't find anyone to let us in. It was kind of comical that all of these people had managed to get in to where we could not. In the amount of time that had passed, I could have walked all the way around the hotel and back in through the front door. With frustration mounting, two paramedics grabbed a ladder off of the fire truck and put it up against the fence. We climbed inside the enclosure just as another guest came out via the pedestrian gate. Murphy's law in action.

The paramedics' ECG machine confirmed what most of us had surmised. The man had died as a result of massive deceleration trauma. He had taken a flying leap out of the hotel window, fallen through a small hardwood tree—Rambo style, and then landed inches from that wrought iron fence that, had he caught a stiff breeze, would have undoubtedly cut him into two pieces and made for a bit more interesting story.

We listened while all the family members moaned and groaned and then I found out that the mysterious blonde was in fact the aforementioned girlfriend. The man had apparently given her the same cryptic call he had given his son. She left abruptly as a combination of the shock of seeing her boyfriend dead and the fact that the man's son had allegedly threatened to kill her for "causing" his dad's suicide.

What makes this story particularly ironic is that on the way out of the hotel, I happened to notice an odd little, tri-fold ad card that was on each of the tables in the pool area. It was one of those cards that tells you what the drink specials are and advertises happy hour and other stuff. This particular card was advertising one of the most peculiar things I have seen yet. It beckoned would-be guests to "Come Celebrate Leap Year."

I don't think that's what they had in mind.

12.3 Heading For The Great Beyond

We have all seen the news reports about Evil that goes on a killing rampage which ultimately concludes with Evil taking its own life. According to the people who study this stuff and then write books about it, the suicide is the inevitable result of the psychopathology that drove them to kill in the first place. It seems as though whatever extreme emotions drive the individual to kill, override the basic instinct that tells him that killing is a bad thing. Then, as time and the situation progresses, Evil becomes more cognizant of the horreineous deeds he has committed. He is not equipped to deal with the impact of that realization and tries to make things right by ending his own life, blah-blah-blah.

The first question that sane people inevitably ask in reference to these situations is, "Why couldn't he have just fast-forwarded to where he kills himself and leave the others out of it?" I guess it's just the nature of the beast. Sane people can't understand it and really shouldn't try.

One of the first times I had the misfortune of witnessing this behavior first-hand was as the result of an ongoing domestic dispute. The female had been trying to leave the male for a while but he wouldn't allow such a grievous violation of his unwritten, testosteronal (my word again - it means "Of or having to do with testosterone and, indirectly, with anything specifically or primarily male.") regulations. This incident was a little creepy because of the way in which it unfolded.

Radio dispatched the call on a prowler trying to break into a residence. I was familiar with the address because of all the previous domestic disputes I had handled there. The dispatcher told us that the prowler was the ex-husband and that the caller was afraid he was coming to kill her as he had threatened to do earlier in the day.

For some unknown reason, this was one of the only times that our radio room personnel have ever kept a caller on the telephone. They should have told her to run out the back but it doesn't really matter now. While several units were all running at top speed to get to the apartment, the dispatcher updated us on the call, "All units be advised that the perpetrator has made entry." (I hope that the reader will excuse this brief, parenthetical rant, but the term "be advised" is one of the single most useless phrases in the entire police language. It has no meaning! If you take the term out of any sentence, the sentence still says the same thing—and says it more quickly.)

A moment or two passed before we were told that the call taker had heard a lot of screaming, a loud bang, and then nothing. When we pulled up to the apartment, Evil was sitting on the front steps with a shotgun in his hand. Before the first officer could even challenge him to drop the weapon, he pointed it at his own face and pulled the trigger.

His body was left in much the same condition as he had left his former significant other. Most of the top of the head was gone. The lower jaw was still there—sort of—with the teeth mostly intact. The skull evaporated into little bitty bits that were sprayed on the wall behind him. Part of one side of his head was left with what looked like the lower portion of the ear still intact. The rest of his head just looked like goo. Varying shades of red white and even a little yellow mixed with the black from the shotgun blast made it hard to tell exactly what was what.

The weird thing for me is that when bodies are that torn up, they don't look real. Maybe it's the side effect of too many gory movies.

12.4 A Bridge To The Afterlife

In the months prior to the writing of this book, in the metro Atlanta area there seemed to be a rash of people wanting to kill themselves by jumping off of highway overpasses. One or two of them were talked down by the police after having caused immense traffic backups that lasted for hours. One of them fell during negotiations and lived to feel an indescribable amount of pain and public ridicule. That's one of the problems with highway overpasses: sometimes they just aren't high enough to guarantee a positive result.

To virtually guarantee success, you have to do what an individual did on our shift one morning at about 4:00 AM. Up until about 3:00 AM that morning we had almost no calls for service and the night was really dragging. Then, in the course of an hour or so, we had a burglary in progress and a couple of foot chases that really taxed our already short-handed shift. The last call (thankfully) of any significance was that 4:00 AM call which was first dispatched as a roadway obstruction.

Dispatch updated us a few minutes later saying that the obstruction was possibly a body. Due to all the other calls working at the time, it took us a little longer than usual to arrive. In the meantime, an officer from another jurisdiction rolled up and confirmed for us that there was indeed a body in the roadway.

That raised the priority of the call a bit and several cars vacated their calls to respond. When we arrived, we discovered the partial remnants of a human being blocking the second lane. As we began diverting traffic and clearing the four lane highway, we found the drag mark. It was a long, intermittent smear of blood and tissue that led back at least a hundred yards to a point directly under the leading edge of an overpass. It was there that we found the point of splattus maximus.

This guy did it right. He walked out onto the bridge over the highway. This particular bridge is one of the few remaining in the area that has only a guard rail about three to four feet high and no fence to deter people from throwing things (like themselves) onto the highway below. Judging from the position where I found his sandals, he stopped just over lane three and slipped off those sandals, leaving them neatly placed next to one another on the bridge sidewalk.

Then he likely watched and waited for a car to come at him in the lane below him. When he saw one, he timed his leap to land him right in front of the approaching vehicle. His plan was executed flawlessly. I imagine that even the Russian judge would have given him a "10". When he hit the pavement he was struck by a tow truck and another vehicle that were responsible for that long and disgusting drag mark. As is usually the case, his head exploded and little bits of brain and skull were among the debris scattered about the roadway. His clothes were mostly ripped away and what was left of his body was mangled and dismembered. I think that an effective way to deter this aberrant behavior would be to have photos of the aftermath of these suicides available for viewing. It is just plain nasty.

This guy did manage to block up traffic during rush hour for almost three hours while we waited for the medical examiner. Who knows, that very well may have been the pinnacle of his life's accomplishments.

12.5 Puddle Of Goo

Maybe I am just a big sissy but the thought of goring myself with a sharp object just really makes me queasy. From my perspective you have to be really gutsy or really sick to pick that as a method of transition from this life to the next. The worst one in recent memory for me is a guy who was suffering from the all too familiar "nobody loves me" syndrome. His girlfriend was leaving him and if he couldn't have her back, then life just wasn't worth living. Whatever.

This guy opted for the wrist cutting method and as is often the case, he waited for his girlfriend to arrive before committing the act. When people do this it is supposed to be some sort of desperate move to prove the depth of one's love for another or some such nonsense.

Anyway, he took a nice long kitchen knife and didn't just cut himself: he took the knife and rammed it all the way through his arm (ouch). Then he wiggled and twisted the knife so violently that he ended up bending the blade. This caused the knife to get stuck between the two bones in his forearm. When we arrived on the scene, the little wooden walkway from the parking lot to the apartment was drenched in partially coagulated blood. It was difficult to walk to the apartment without getting the stuff all over our boots.

When we got to the open door to the apartment, our "victim", who depending on your point of view could also be the "perpetrator", was lying (not laying) on the kitchen floor in a puddle of his own goo. He still had the knife in his arm and was turning that queer shade of bluish white that a person gets just prior to the transition.

Paramedics bandaged him up and rushed him off to the hospital and the last I heard, the guy actually lived. We were all amazed.

12.6 Pretzel Boy

Most suicides are intentional acts. When I classify something as a suicide, I generally go a step farther than the average Joe. In my opinion, if you do something that is really stupid and it results in your death, whether that was the intended outcome or not, it is still a suicide. Consequently, many police chases are in fact suicide attempts and some of them are extraordinarily successful.

One such pursuit that comes to mind started when one of our officers attempted to make a traffic stop on a driver that he suspected was operating under the influence. As soon as the officer activated his emergency equipment, the driver made his intentions quite clear. Because of his level of intoxication, not only was low speed driving a challenge for him, but high speed navigation of the winding two lane road on which he chose to begin his flight from police was a prodigious task indeed.

I had a trainee riding with me at the time and I thought it would be a good experience for him if we got in the back of the line of police cars and just followed and watched. I gave him a running commentary while we brought up the rear. Because of the terrain, we initially didn't have to exceed the speed limit to keep up with the pack but after about fifteen minutes, Evil found his way to a wide open road with very few curves and even less traffic. He wasted no time accelerating to a dangerous speed. The manifestations of his intoxication, in the form of erratic driving, increased exponentially in relation to his speed.

When he had gotten up to about 70 or 80 mph, he actually opened his car door and leaned out of it, looking back at us and taunting us with words that were lost beneath the deafening roar of wind and engines. He drifted toward the left side of the road and just before impacting the curb, he turned forward and abruptly corrected his trajectory.

It wasn't long before he decided to lean back out the door again. Again he drifted left but this time when he corrected, he did it too sharply and lost control. The car careened one way and then the other before he lost control completely and slid sideways toward the right side of the road. The point where he left the roadway happened to coincide with the placement of a large utility pole. The result was a violent impact that bent the car down the middle and flipped it over.

The car landed on its roof and the unrestrained driver was tossed around the inside like an egg in a blender. When all the police cars came to a stop, we converged on what was left of Evil. He was conscious and was still cursing us and yelling and screaming. We could tell by the position of his limbs in relation to the rest of his body that at the very least he had a broken back. He was upside down in the car with his legs twisted around him like a pretzel. Despite his agony he still had the presence of mind to voice his contempt for law enforcement.

As a reward for his actions that evening, the Good Lord allowed him to suffer in complete agony for a couple of hours before he finally succumbed to his injuries and met his hard earned demise.

Do I feel sorry for him?

Absolutely not! He made a decision and suffered the consequences. For the loved ones he may have left behind, that's a different story. They did nothing to deserve the pain that he likely inflicted upon them, assuming of course that someone like that had loved ones. Compassion is a valuable commodity that I do not distribute on a whim. It is something that should be reserved for those who actually deserve it, not cheapened by or wasted on those who would scoff at it.

CHAPTER THIRTEEN
Let The Games Begin

In the summer of 1996, the metro Atlanta area was host to the Summer Olympic Games. Our city had spent years building and preparing. Law enforcement and private corporations feverishly worked to pave the way for what we hoped would be an uneventful yet exciting experience for all the world to enjoy.

Because of all the heightened security, most of the local law enforcement agencies had gone to twelve hour shifts with one day off per week. My particular department had shifts running from 7:00 AM to 7:00 PM and vice versa. The third shift that was a "floating" shift that ran from 2:00 PM to 2:00 AM. Because of my relative seniority, I asked for and was assigned to work that floating shift. The other two shifts were tasked with handling calls for service and general police work. The floating shift was granted free reign to handle anything that could be classified as a "special detail" and would assist the other two shifts with their work if and when it became necessary.

Because of all the cancelled off-days and all the subsequent police that were on the street, things were relatively quiet. For once in my career, I saw enough police working in my jurisdiction to handle virtually anything. We literally had five patrol cars routinely showing up on even the most mundane of calls. We were tripping over one another trying to find something to do that was law enforcement related.

My supervisors told me to think of some kind of a special detail to go on to justify my existence and then to organize and execute that detail. I was at a loss. The only complaints we had recently received were from residents near a county park who were tired of all of the "homosexual activity" going on there after dark. Allegedly, there were lots of men who liked to hang out in the park and have sex with each other in public. As a natural side effect of that not-so-natural behavior, random articles of clothing, prophylactic devices (used and unused) and adult media materials had been left haphazardly all over the park. Understandably, people were hesitant about bringing their children into this environment.

Thus, my brilliant idea was to set up surveillance on the park and arrest any violators. The first part of the operation was to find a suitable surveillance point from which we could watch and learn. Initially, we wanted to make sure that there was actually a problem. Next we wanted to formulate a plan for dealing with that problem should it exist. What I was about to see still astonishes me to this day.

I will try to be as succinct as possible in describing the events I witnessed at that little county park where I used to play as a child. The parking lot of this park is parallel to the roadway and has about fifteen parking spaces. There is an interstate highway that runs parallel to that road on the back side of the park. The interstate is at the top of a steep embankment that is at least fifty feet high and covered with generations of kudzu vines. There is a small creek that runs through the center of the park from the front to the back and then turns left. It runs along the back of the park for a few yards before it makes a gradual left turn and runs out of the park.

Most of the park is dirt or grass except for a strip in the rear that has heavy growth of underbrush and kudzu. For the more shy sex offenders, someone had pounded trails through the brush in the rear of the park that, because of the dense vegetation, resembled tunnels. In these tunnels one could conceal his activities from the eyes of the general public.

We watched the park intermittently for two nights to establish the patterns that the target offenders used to satisfy their rather strange urges. What we saw was, like so many human behaviors, as predictable as clockwork. It showed such a degree of planning and execution that it made me wonder if they had a magazine or monthly meetings to establish the protocol for these bizarre encounters.

A "hungry" man would pull up in the parking lot and sit in his car. Most of the time, these were the "catchers". That means that they would be on the receiving end of any bodily fluid exchange. The "pitcher" would then pull up in the parking lot next to one of the parked catchers. They would eye each other for a minute and if one of them saw something that he liked, he would get out of the car and meander into the park, all the while turning to give that knowing glance to the anonymous, amorous other.

If the other was interested, then he would follow the first guy into the park where they would pick a nice dark spot to do their dirty deed. Consummation of the deal rarely took more than 5 minutes and little time was wasted in getting down to business.

At some times during our surveillance, there were so many couples in the park assumably doing the nasty, that we couldn't get close enough, quickly enough to catch one in the act without spooking all of the others. Up to this point, we had a lot of suspicious behavior but no concrete evidence of any crime other than the misdemeanor, non-arrestable offense of being in the park after hours.

The first incident that I actually witnessed that was primary evidence of an arrestable offense was to me a bit disturbing. Being a devout "hetero", up to that point in my life I had never seen two men engage in anything more than a kiss and to me that was creepy enough. I would like to point out at this point that I think homosexuality is wrong, immoral, sinful or whatever other word you want to use. I also understand that we live in a free country and I fully support anyone's right to engage in consensual sex of any kind with another adult in the privacy of their own home, office or hotel etc. without government interference or intervention.

I am not "homo-phobic" and I don't hate gay people. Their sin is no better or worse than anyone else's. I have several good friends who are gay. That's their business, not mine. I do reserve the first amendment right to poke fun at them just like I poke fun at a lot of other people (including myself) for a lot of other reasons. I can dish it out and I can take it. My only professional problem with their behavior is that it was being carried out not just in a public park but in one where children play and where I had (up until that day) fond memories of playing as a child.

But anyway—the first incident followed the aforementioned screenplay to the letter. The participants did their little mating dance in the parking lot and headed into the park to seal the deal. The two "men" walked to within twenty feet of my hiding place and were standing in the dark but were still right out in the center of the open park. The pitcher stopped in his tracks and as he pulled his shorts down to his thighs, the catcher assumed his position on his knees. Just as penis contacted mouth, another car pulled into the parking lot at such an angle that its headlights struck the little woodland fairies almost dead on. With that, pants went up and the players scurried away.

That was the first and I am sorry to say only the next to the last time that I would see something that disturbed me in that unique way. I still get what can only be described as a "fag chill" every time I think about it. I had seen all I needed to begin making cases. I did not have to wait long before the same song, different verse, was sung by two new enthusiasts. As I said earlier, they were as dependable as Old Faithful and I knew almost exactly how much time it would take for the heinous act to commence.

I gave them about three minutes to get fully involved, gave the signal to my compatriots, and we converged on the area of the park where we thought the two turtle doves were nesting. As I approached the wood line near the rear of the park, I could make out the image of a man. I illuminated his form with my 50,000 candlepower Mag-lite flashlight and what I saw was the second most disturbing sight I have ever seen in a public park. There he was with his pants around his ankles and his big, fish-belly-white butt staring at me with that vertical smile that both stunned and mocked me simultaneously.

At the appearance of my light, the catcher sprinted from his kneeling position right into one of those brushy tunnels (an ironic metaphor indeed). The pitcher was obviously a victim of his position and in the time it took for him to pull his pants up, I had him handcuffed. The other two officers went off in pursuit of the catcher. I called for the uniform cars to respond to our location and secured my captive inside of the port-a perp (prisoner transport vehicle). I then went to join the other officers in the hunt for the catcher. We beat the bushes for several minutes and even walked through the shallow creek looking for Mr. Goodbar. (A Somewhat obscure yet deep and multi-faceted metaphor referring to the 1970's movie starring Diane Keaton. The implications are way too numerous for a parenthetical note.)

I was a little frustrated, I admit, but I was tired of looking for the little dirtbag so I stopped on the bank overlooking the creek where I thought he might be hiding. I then yelled out into the darkness, "Alright you stupid little shit. I'll give you thirty seconds to show yourself. After that, when I find you, and I will find you, I am going to beat your sorry little ass."

This is one of those times when the bark has to be worse than the intended bite. Of course I would not have done anything outside of the law to the guy; that is not my way. I am one of the most non-violent people you will ever meet. Whether I like you, agree with you, despise you or down right hate your guts, I will not assault you unjustifiably no matter what. Why would I risk my life, my livelihood, and all my personal possessions by smackin' some scumbag whether he deserves it or not? Sometimes you have to posture to accomplish the task at hand.

About one third of my ultimatum time passed before I heard this precious little whimpering voice call out, "Um…I'm over here sir. Please don't hurt me. I'll come out now."

He came out, no pun intended, and I lived up to my end of the bargain and quietly secured him for his ride to the jail.

When the two gentlemen made their first court appearance, the judge asked both of their attorneys for psychiatric evaluations of their clients in exchange for the opportunity to have the cases handled on the county level rather than in superior court. The accused complied. The pitcher's attorney went first. He provided the requested analysis and then spoke on his client's behalf.

"Your honor, my client is a well respected businessman and is a deacon in his church. He is a father and devoted family man. He has never done this type of thing before and promises that he never will again. He has never been arrested before and has been so adversely affected by this experience that he will never do anything to put himself in this position again. Though he has not been tested recently for HIV, he is confident that he has not been exposed to the virus."

The catcher's attorney then chimed in.

"Your honor, my client has led a troubled life. He was divorced a few years ago and hasn't been able to find steady employment since. He comes from a broken home with a history of child abuse. He has been in and out of jail for minor offenses and wants to get counseling for his self-destructive behavior. He has a substance abuse problem, he is currently homeless and on a recent doctor's visit, he was told that he is positive for HIV."

Pitcher gulped and turned pale.

13.2 Things That Go Boom

While we were assigned to twelve hour shifts, some officers were assigned to work certain Olympic venues while some of us were, as I said previously, assigned to regular police type duties. On our off-day every week, most of us took advantage of the surplus of extra security jobs and worked for one of the plethora of private corporations that were offering $35-$75 per hour for police officers. My chosen extra job was for the Coca-Cola Company at the Olympic City working from 7:00 pm to 7:00 am securing the park. The front gate of the Olympic City was directly across the street from the front gate of Centennial Olympic park.

On the night of July 17th, our worst fears materialized when TWA flight 800 was shot down of the coast of New York City. We all immediately suspected terrorism and most of the evidence forthcoming in the first few days served to confirm what we already knew. Despite the White House spin over the next few years that served to discredit the over seven hundred eyewitnesses and reams of evidence proving that a missile or other planned explosion had caused the demise of that flight and all aboard, the media and the numbed American public ultimately succumbed to the Clinton Party line that it was some freak mechanical malfunction—yeah right.

That airline crash was the first in history to be investigated primarily by the FBI rather than the NTSB. That's sort of like hiring your accountant to do your brain surgery. They did about as good a job in that investigation as they did in pinning the Centennial Olympic Park bombing on Richard Jewel. The only thing we can say for sure is that they tried. That type of investigative prowess is why most police officers I know who have ever come into contact with the FBI, know that the initials actually stand for Famous But Incompetent (or if you prefer—Freakin' Bunch of Idiots). For anyone interested in knowing just how incompetent that organization was in respect to the flight 800 crash, I recommend that you read Jack Cashill's book, "First Strike". It offers an in depth, well researched look at the downing of TWA Flight 800.

But I digress...on the evening of Friday, July 26th, all hell broke loose in Atlanta when the infamous Centennial Park bomb exploded. Needless to say, we were on extremely high alert when I reported for duty the next night to the Olympic City. The parks were all closed and the Red Cross was there feeding and assisting all the law enforcement that had converged on the location. I would like to commend them for the wonderful job that they did at the scene.

Over the course of the days and weeks that followed the Centennial Park bombing, we in the law enforcement community were continually privy to "inside information" concerning the whereabouts of additional devices. The term "device", of course, refers to a bomb. Bomb threats became a common occurrence after the Centennial Park bomb. Literally hundreds of them came into the 911 center each day. Very few of them were made public and the vast majority of them were false alarms. For those of us who were curious, we would turn to our radios and talk with our friends from different agencies to determine which bomb threats were real and which were unfounded. From there we would find out which devices were genuine and which, if any, were merely hoaxes.

It amazed me then and it amazes me to this day how many devices were located and "confirmed" by my law enforcement cohorts, but then never released to the media. The devices that the media did find out about were declared to be fake or imitation bombs built to scare people. I'll freely admit that my sources are second hand but they were quite reliable and I would stand behind them 100% until shown positive proof to the contrary.

From listening to certain police channels, I heard of at least four confirmed explosive devices that had to be disarmed or detonated. One was in a MARTA (Metro Atlanta Rapid Transit Authority) station. It was reported as a fake device but I listened to the radio traffic as they were disarming it. Rarely is there much excitement over the disarming of a fake device. Judging by what I heard on the police radio, that device was no fake.

Another device was allegedly located in a downtown hotel and still another was located in somewhere in Underground Atlanta but I cannot recall exactly where. (Underground Atlanta is a commercial district and a popular location for tourists.) I never heard news reports of any of these. For all of those conspiracy theorists out there, I would like to add that no one ever told us not to talk about these devices. Nothing was ever said at all.

As for bomb stories, the best one I have occurred on one Sunday morning. I ask the reader to forgive my failing memory here because I cannot remember on exactly which Sunday this next event occurred though I am reasonably certain that it was in the early morning hours of the 4th of August.

After midnight, all of the officers assigned to the Olympic City were finding their own little dark corner to secure. Some of us would go off by ourselves to check our eyelids for cracks or read a book, while others would gather in groups to play cards or talk about whatever was on our minds. Others would wander aimlessly through the park until they decided to join one of the other two ranks. Two or three select officers would have golf cart detail and would just ride around the park checking on all the other officers. All in all it was a pretty easy and uneventful job.

All that changed when, in the wee hours of the morning, our radios crackled to life with the garbled screams of one of our security coordinators. She was driving a golf cart through the center of the park screaming like a banshee.

"Everybody get out of the park!!!! There's a bomb, there's a bomb! Get out, get out! Use the Simpson Street exit. Leave now!!!" Most veteran officers tend to be an unexcitable bunch and despite the frantic yelling of the security boss, we all slowly emerged from our cubby holes and walked un-urgently toward the designated exit.

Once outside the gates in what we deemed to be a safe zone, we regrouped and sat and waited for additional information. Over the course of the next couple of hours, I watched a little TV and played games on my Sega Game Gear and listened to the sporadic radio traffic concerning the car bomb that was located on the street between the Olympic City and the Centennial Park. Somebody's joint task force bomb squad something or other set up barricades and then allegedly diffused the bomb with a well placed 12 gauge shotgun slug. The device was then quietly carted away by the powers that be and no news report that I am aware of ever uttered a single word about the incident.

We were given the 'all clear' signal and filtered back into

the park to finish out our shift, securing whatever corner we had grown fond of over the course of our employment there. Just before going back into the park I realized that one of my buddies, who was last seen securing the darkness near the front gate, was nowhere to be found. I asked if anyone had seen him and no one had.

Not wanting to cause a panic at that late hour, I went looking for him by myself. I went to the front gate and way back in the darkest corner of the structure that supported the entrance and all of its sign work, I found him. He was leaned back in a chair with his eyes closed and his head sunken into his chest, snoring loudly enough to register on any nearby seismometers.

I started laughing and went to wake him up. He asked what was so funny and I told him that the rest of us had spent the last two hours outside of the opposite side of the park hiding from the car bomb while the bomb squad blew it up with a shotgun. He looked at me rather incredulously and said something like, "Nah uh. You're messin' with me."

I said, "Damn son, if you could sleep through all that, I guess the bomb wouldn't have bothered you anyway."

To this day I still think he thinks I was joking.

CHAPTER FOURTEEN
Flim-Flams, Cons, and Scams

One of my favorite types of crimes is the flim-flam. 'Flim-Flam' is synonymous with scam or confidence scheme, but I just like to say 'Flim-Flam'. It's fun for my tongue. Simply put, the crime is fraud regardless of what name you give it. The reason it is one of my favorite crimes is that unlike the average criminal, the flim-flammer/scammer Evil has to be somewhat creative to perpetrate his particular crime. Perhaps that is why con men are one of the few criminal types who are called "artists". Webster's dictionary gives several meanings for the word 'art'.

1. An occupation requiring knowledge or skill.
2. Creativity of man as distinguished from the world of nature.
3. Creative work or its principles; a making or doing of things that display form, beauty, and unusual perception.

In the truest sense of the word, the accomplished confidence man indeed practices an art. As long as there are people alive anywhere in the universe, they will be developing crafty new ways of deceiving and exploiting one another as well as reviving age-old, time-honored schemes developed and implemented by long forgotten practitioners of their sacred art. The nuances for each conceivable scam are in themselves innumerable.

There are two main reasons why the majority of flim-flams are successful. The primary reason is greed. People seem to have a natural tendency to be greedy. They want to take shortcuts. They always want something for nothing. They want the prize without having to run the race. They want to enjoy the harvest without the burden of plowing or planting. It is just another one of those aspects of human nature that certain individuals have chosen to exploit.

The second reason, whether working in concert with the first or as a solo act, is sheer stupidity. Stupidity is nature's great entertainer. Even the smartest person in the world has a moment or two over the course of his or her life when he or she commits an act of stupidity. Thankfully, there seems to be no shortage of it.

One of the less creative flim-flams that has been common throughout my career is where the flim-flammer approaches someone who looks like a gullible mark in a parking lot. For the purposes of this chapter, let's just call him Mark. Usually he is in the parking lot of a large department store or grocery store. Often Mark is a senior citizen who is much more likely to be trusting of a stranger. Evil will produce a wallet or an envelope containing something of transferable value like cash, money orders, or lottery tickets purported to have hit the jackpot.

Evil then tells Mark something like, "If you help me, I'll split all this money with you." That's when the greed kicks in. Mark sees all this free money and his eyes start rolling around in his head and his brain immediately short circuits.

"Sure. I'll help you. What do you need me to do Mr. Kind Stranger who wants to give me something for nothing?"

Evil, posing as Mr. Kind Stranger, then says something like, "I verified that this is the winning lottery ticket but I don't have time to cash it in. If you'll take me to the bank and give me...$5000, I'll give you this multi-million dollar ticket." Or he says, "I don't have a bank account and when I called the bank, they told me that to open a new account with cash, (or money orders or checks or whatever) they need a corresponding amount of cash from an established account holder. If you'll just withdraw…say…$5000, you can make an additional $5000 for doing absolutely nothing."

Even though many schemes of this type really make no sense at all when you stop and put a little grey matter to work on them, many people still get possessed by the greed demon and do some pretty stupid things—like give a total stranger large sums of money on the promise that he will return the favor. If it sounds too good to be true then it probably is.

14.2 Pigeon Drop

Another common flim-flam has Evil walking into a local business, claiming to have lost something of extreme value, either monetary or sentimental. Evil asks Mark if he has seen the valuable object in question and of course Mark says, "No."

Evil then says, "Here's my name and phone number. If anyone finds it I will give them a huge reward (like $500)." Then Evil leaves. The phone number left is usually to a nearby payphone and Evil normally does not use his real name.

A few minutes later, Evil #2 comes up to the same Mark and says, "Hi Mark. Look what I just found in the parking lot." Then Evil #2 produces the item for which Evil #1 had promised the reward.

Mark then says, "Hey, a customer lost that and is offering a big reward if you just call him/her."

Evil #2 says, "I am in a big hurry, Mark. Can you just give me a large sum of money equal to …say… half the reward amount and I'll leave this here with you."

Mark might sometimes call the phone number to confirm that the reward is on the way. Evil #1 will be waiting to reassure him. Mark then gives half of the reward money to Evil #2 and that's the end of the scam. Mark loses again.

14.3 "Take" Card

The first two flim-flams required at least the appearance of something valuable. What about the con man who has nothing like that but needs some quick cash. Many of our homeless people will dig through trash cans or sift through unlocked vehicles in large parking lots looking for used gift cards. By gift cards, I mean those little plastic store credit cards you can buy at places like Home Depot, Wal-Mart, Macy's etc that give you a preset amount of spendable "cash".

Evil will take the card to Mark and say something like, "Hey buddy. I have $53 left on this gift card but they won't give me cash in the store and I left my wallet at home," or some other such nonsense.

"If you'll give me $20, I'll give you this $53 gift card and you can go buy some stuff."

You would be amazed at the number of people who will not think long before they abjectly surrender the requested amount of cash without even taking the simple step of walking into the store to have the card verified. That ugly greed demon strikes again.

14.4 Box O' Rocks

Then there's the guy on the street corner who is selling VCRs, TVs, stereos or the like. He has a car full of boxes or maybe only one or two. One of the boxes is open and has the electronic item that is for sale inside and exposed. He offers the item to Mark for a really great price and even lets him examine the item at will. Mark may be thinking to himself that this item is stolen but figures no one will ever know, so why not get a brand new one for such a good price?

After a little deliberation, Mark hands over the requested amount of cash and gets a nice new sealed box with the promised item packed neatly inside. Evil speeds away and when Mark opens the box, he finds nothing but a brick or some rocks used to approximate the weight of the item he thought he was buying. Poor, poor Mark.

14.5 Change Up

Here's one that gets a little confusing. It can be so confusing to some people that Mark often never even realizes he has been flim-flammed. The con game may have several names but I like to call it the "change-up".

Evil enters a store. Any kind of store will do. He buys something for a small amount of money and pays with a large bill. For example let's say that he buys a pack of gum for seventy nine cents and pays with a $10 bill. The cashier gives him back $9 and change.

Evil then says, "You know, Mark, I really don't want all these little bills. How 'bout I give you the bills back plus a dollar and you give me the $10 bill back?"

Mark says, "Sure. No problem."

Evil must get Mark to give the $10 bill back first or at least simultaneously. Evil will usually be engaging Mark in conversation to keep his mind off of what is going on. Evil then gives the nine dollars he got in change plus the $10 bill that Mark just handed him. He hopes that Mark will count the money and realize that he now has $19 instead of $10. If Mark doesn't count the cash, Evil will prompt him to do so.

Mark is now holding the $19 (nine of which belongs to Evil and a $10 bill belonging to the store). Whether Mark catches the error on his own or because Evil asked him to do a recount, Evil still says, "Thanks for catching that gross error on my part there Mark. I must have included a $10 bill instead of a $1 bill. I tell you what. Here's another dollar bill to make it an even twenty." Evil hands over the dollar and asks for a $20 bill in return.

Mark complies and Evil nets ten bucks. This can work with larger sums of money as well but gets even more complicated and difficult to pull off. The last time I took a report on this type of flim-flam was at a fast food restaurant. The store manager told me that he was the one who got scammed. He knew because he was "...from up North where they do this stuff a lot." He told me that he knew the guy was running a scam on him but he thought he was good enough to turn the scam around on Evil. After counting the drawer he realized that he was not as smart as he thought.

14.6 Where's The Beef?

This next flim-flam is kind of unique but the principle could be applied in many different circumstances. This craftily woven scheme took a rather astute steakhouse manager several months to unravel. He knew that someone in his employ was stealing either money or food, but he did not know which. He started looking over his list of suspects and narrowed it down to one or two members of the wait staff.

He watched the waiters intently for several weeks before he finally figured out how they were committing the thefts. The two men were roommates and like most college age kids, they had a computer. They spent several weeks studying their orders every night and determined that certain combinations of food orders seemed to appear with some regularity.

They stole some of the restaurant's blank order tickets and managed to get a printer or program that closely mimicked the cash register printer. Then they would use the blank tickets and printer to print up several tickets for each of those commonly recurring order combinations.

Each waiter would then wear two aprons to work. He would keep the bogus tickets in the under apron and would wait until one of the orders he had a preprinted ticket for was made by one of his customers. The orders didn't have to be exact because the waiter could always tell the customer that he "comped" a certain item and that is why it wasn't on the bill. Obviously, he had to make sure that everything on the ticket had actually been ordered to avoid a potential plot-uncovering complaint from the customer.

The waiter would then leave the bogus ticket on the table and would come back to collect the payment which he would then put in his pocket. Since the order had never been entered in the restaurant computer it never showed up as a loss on the register. If a credit card was used, he could process the order and take an equivalent amount of cash out of the register without any risk of coming up short.

Anyone needing a receipt could take the original. Evil didn't need it anymore anyway. Management estimated that over the course of the investigation, the two waiters made off with close to $5000.

14.7 Will Work For Food

One of the more common scams is the ubiquitous "Will Work For Food" scam. I think we have all seen the guys at the end of the exit ramp or on the side of the road with the signs that try to play on our kindness and compassion. Don't be fooled—the vast majority of these people have no desire to work for food or for money. They just want a handout and usually they get plenty of them.

There used to be an old lady who would show up periodically who learned how to work this type scam better than anyone I have ever heard of. She changed her sign to read "Need bus fare to Richmond". It was a new variation on an old theme. There were so many beggars with the other signs or that were just asking for money outright that she had to come up with something new. The funny thing was that her sign was part truth.

She would sit by the road, day after day, with her sign and whenever the police finally decided to run her off, they would discover that she had huge amounts of cash in her purse. I actually asked her how much she averaged in a day and she said that $200 was usually the low and she sometimes made over $500 in one day. She freely admitted to us what she was doing and actually seemed to be pretty proud of her resourcefulness and success. When she worked the area for a week or two she would actually go hop a bus to Richmond or any other of a number of cities that she had on her route. She would run the same scam in city after city and would eventually return back to our area.

A local journalist ran a story on how she actually toured the country using her unique style of panhandling. She made a substantial living working the exit ramps of cities all over North America. One day she just disappeared and I have no idea what happened to her. I also never gave the lady a dime because I knew that she was con artist.

I would be much more likely to donate to an honest loser who had a sign that said, "Please give me money because I'm too lazy to work". Hey, at least he's being honest—and that counts for something in my book.

People you see on the roadside soliciting assistance are very rarely actually in need. We have a large number of individuals who have another variation of the scam that has not been quite as successful as the old lady's, but it is close. They will usually stop their car on an exit ramp or at an intersection and pretend to be broken down. They flag down cars asking for gas money or taxi fare because their kid is in the hospital or some other such nonsense designed to pull on your heart strings.

If someone's car breaks down right at an intersection or at the top of a ramp or some other place where cars have to stop because of traffic, I would be wary. Murphy's Law says if you are going to break down, you are going to do it at the least advantageous point, not the most. Always be suspicious of these people. While usually they are just looking for a handout, they have been known to commit the occasional armed robbery or carjacking.

14.8 Cajones

My last flim-flam is a rare bird indeed but was creative enough for me to want to include it here. It shows more "cajones" than most of the other ones I have come across because it involves impersonating a police officer.

Evil will approach Mark in the parking lot of a bank. He will flash a badge and/or identification claiming to be a police officer or bank security or something similar. He then explains to Mark that one of the bank tellers is suspected of passing counterfeit money. He enlists Mark's help in a sting operation that will help to bring this heinous bank teller to justice.

He tells Mark that he needs him to go back into the bank and withdraw some money, making sure that he uses the particular teller in question. Mark is supposed to bring the money out to Evil to have it inspected. Evil assures Mark that he will be reimbursed.

Mark complies and returns with the requested amount of cash. It is usually a fairly large amount since most counterfeiters don't bother with small bills. Mark hands the cash over to the "investigator" who either takes off running or, if he is more subtle, tells Mark he is going somewhere to test the cash to see if it's real or not. Either way, that's the last Mark sees of his money.

The bottom line is that you just can't blindly trust people when it's your money involved. Don't be afraid to ask questions and always ask for proof. Don't take proof from the suspected Evil, seek it out on your own.

As police officers, we have to try not to make fun of Mark. Usually it's really not his fault and he is probably a pretty good guy. We have to be aware of how these things work and learn how to recognize these crimes when they occur.

We should also be aware that when we initiate contact with certain people, they may be wary of us as well, especially if they are smart. Take for instance a loud noise call or a call to check on the welfare of someone. They may refuse to open the door for you. That lone female you are trying to make a traffic stop on in the middle of the night may keep driving until she finds a "safe" place to stop. Instead of getting mad at these people and threatening them or arresting them, help them to take whatever steps will make them comfortable that you are in fact the police. Don't let Evil get the best of you in the process though.

CHAPTER FIFTEEN
Baron Von Munchausen

Karl Friedrich Hieronymous von Munchausen, commonly known as Baron von Munchausen, lived from 1720 to 1797. He worked his way up through the ranks of a Russian cavalry regiment and retired as a captain circa 1760. His main claim to fame was that he was a renowned story teller. He had a knack for spinning magnificent tales of adventure. As the story goes, a collection of such tales entitled Baron Munchausen's Narrative of His Marvelous Travels and Campaigns in Russia was published in the early 1780s with the Baron himself as the purported author. There seems to be some dispute as to the origin of many of the tales attributed to the "Baron of Lies" but legend had already cemented his place in history. Over time, other authors built upon his style of exaggerated stories to the point where the name Munchausen became synonymous with a teller of tall tales.

It is from this particular reputation that the Baron was catapulted to a completely new realm of relevance when somewhere around the late 1980s, his name was applied to a psychiatric disorder. Munchausen Syndrome was the term coined to refer to someone who repeatedly fabricates a particular physical illness and seeks treatment at multiple facilities for his ailment. Munchausen Syndrome By Proxy, or MSBP, is a variant of this mental malfunction whereby the nutbag with a serious screw loose manufactures illness or injury not on himself but on a helpless child.

Common manifestations of this "syndrome", which as far

as I am concerned is just a euphemism for Evil, include physically injuring a child to make it look like an illness or accident, using poison or chemicals to induce an illness, or simply lying about symptoms to get someone to provide unnecessary treatment. I can only guess that it is a way for these lunatics to feel needed or important, or to get attention from someone, as if that would give some sort of sick validity to their twisted, miserable existence.

To ask why someone does something like this is, to me, an exercise in futility. Treatment lies in the purview of the doctors and is not my concern. What does concern me is that these people need to be identified and quarantined so that they cannot perpetrate their peculiar Evil on the most innocent of our society.

Throughout a large portion of my career, I worked a beat that was the home to a children's hospital. As a teenager, I did volunteer work with this same hospital through the Boy Scouts and watched the facility grow and prosper from then through the present day. The hospital does wonderful work and I am proud to be a part of the community it serves. This same hospital is where I got my introduction to the legendary Baron.

Security at the hospital called 911 to request an officer at the scene for some type of investigation. It was the sort of thing that would be too complicated to try to explain to a 911 operator so they just called it child abuse. When I got there, I was ushered into a small, out of the way room crammed with radio equipment, security monitors, recording devices and computers. It was there that I met in a closed door session with a social worker and the head of hospital security.

They gave me a crash course in MSBP and explained that there was a woman who had brought her child in for treatment of a head injury. This same woman had brought her toddler into this same hospital an inordinately large number of times for various reasons over the course of his short and tortured life. Hospital personnel had suspected MSBP when she had the child admitted, so they put the woman and her child into a room that had a covert camera that was used to 'monitor' the mother and child.

Before explaining further, the social worker just said, "You need to watch the tape."

With that she started the machine. What I saw next made my blood boil. I watched as this mother (additional expletive implied) sat calmly with her child in the wee hours of the morning. The child slept soundly in its crib. The mother got up and stood over the crib. She was stroking her child lovingly and looking at it in a way that most mothers do. That demeanor changed in the blink of an eye when she balled up her fist and struck the child three times in its head as hard as she could.

As quickly as it came, the demon that possessed her left and she scooped up her little angel from the crib and began coddling and consoling it. I took a deep breath and made sure that I had quelled the rage within me before I confiscated the tape and asked to be escorted to the mother's location. Without a word I picked her up out of her chair and handcuffed her, giving the toddler over to the social worker. I escorted the "loving" mother out to the patrol car and sat her in the back seat.

She still feigned ignorance of why she was being taken away so I confronted her with what I had seen on the tape. She was overcome by an eerie calm before she broke out into tears.

"I don't know why I did it. I love my child. Please don't take her away from me. She's all I have."

"If you really do love her," I said, "then you should be begging me to take her away from you."

Working near that hospital afforded me many more opportunities to 'meet the Baron'. It never got any easier for me and sometimes it got much harder. I saw parents who had allegedly blistered their children with acid or drain cleaner, parents who poisoned their own children with medicines or household chemicals. There seemed to be no end to the ways people could think of to hurt their kids.

There is one incident in particular that sticks out in my mind as the most hideous of them all, perhaps because of my own aversion to needles. In a story that started in much the same way as the first one in this chapter, I found myself again crammed into that little room watching a security tape. I watched as a small baby slept in a hospital crib. There were little stuffed animals all over the room and all the things you might expect to find around the crib of a child who was loved and cared for by its parents.

The baby was sleeping soundly in the hollow safety of the strange hospital crib. Much like the first mother, this mother swooned over her child as he slept. Again, she looked just as the first mother had and as several had since. Then, the Evil struck. She reached into a small cloth bag, or maybe it was a purse, and she pulled out a small hypodermic needle. She looked around as if to check to see if anyone may have been watching and then she gripped the needle tightly in hand and furiously jabbed it into one of the baby's ears.

One..., two..., three times she thrust that needle into that baby's ear. I thought for sure she had to have pierced its brain considering the fervor with which she rammed it into the skull. I literally came out of my chair. In fact, every time I think of this incident to this day it makes me wince.

In retrospect, it was a good thing that the room where the mother was waiting for the doctors to report on her baby's condition was so far from the security room. The walk there gave me time to regain my composure and kept me from exacting some much needed and much deserved revenge on that pathetic excuse for a human being.

There are still and will likely always be people who will make excuses for criminals. It seems to have become the American way of thinking. In the growing absence of any moral anchor, things that we know to be universal truths are being bastardized, prostituted and flipped topsy turvy. Up has become down, left has become right, right has become wrong, good is now bad, perpetrators are victims and victims, somehow, are now perpetrators.

CHAPTER SIXTEEN
A Garbage Slide You Say?

I couldn't let an entire book go by without dedicating a page (or seven) to one of my trademark social commentaries. That is what this chapter is for and I hope you enjoy it. If you're not into those types of things, you may feel free to close the book now.

In the summer of the year 2000, the weather in the Philippines was exceptionally rainy. News reports indicated that as many as three hundred people died as a result of a rain-induced garbage slide in a small town near Manila. As many as two hundred shanties were buried beneath the collapsing garbage, virtually wiping out an entire town. Continued rainfall caused flooding in the region where search teams focused their efforts, increasing the threat of infection and making rescue attempts difficult if not impossible.

Now, what struck me as most odd was not that an entire town could actually be wiped out by the collapse of a pile of trash but rather the interview with one of the survivors that aired on international television. Through an interpreter, (it is no surprise that anyone who lives in an area where their life can be threatened by other people's trash is not likely to be multilingual) one of the surviving inhabitants of the doomed settlement was asked a fairly perfunctory question. The question was, "Do you plan to move now that your home has been destroyed."

The answer to that question still amazes me to this day. The functional Filipino equivalent of Oscar the Grouch said quite frankly, "If I need to move, the government will move me."

Never in my life before or since that time have I seen someone who so epitomizes the communist way of thinking (even though the government in the Philippines is not communist). The party chairman would be proud of this mindless little drone. This woman had become so dependent upon the government to run her life for her that she was incapable of making even the simplest decision about her own life or death. Not only would she live in a place where garbage could fall on her and kill her but she would not even consider trying to leave without government approval and subsequent assistance.

With my mouth agape, I started thinking. What I realized was that many people in my own country are slowly but surely adopting that same paradigm. Everywhere you turn you see more and more people who are increasingly dependent on government programs. We have senior citizens who had their entire lives to save for their retirement but who then bitch and moan about not getting enough money from the government to pay their rent. We have single mothers who have multiple children by multiple fathers but never consider actually working for a living.

Why should they? They can lie (or maybe even lay) on their backs with their legs spread, not doing a damn thing productive and our tax money will pay to make sure they have a roof over their heads, beer to drink and diapers for the little bastards they keep squirting out. They need to do nothing except fulfill their most primal desires and the taxpayers will foot the bill. We have perfectly capable individuals who, because of their own chemical dependencies or their sheer laziness, refuse to do anything except suck up my hard earned tax money.

Though they shouldn't be, they are allowed to vote in increasing numbers and they generally don't vote for anyone who is going to eliminate their precious, life-sustaining entitlement programs, thereby requiring them to become productive. These are the people who repeat political sound bytes and propaganda lies as if they were the gospel truth. These are the people who are easily brainwashed into toeing the party line with as much control over their own minds as Pavlov's dogs had on their salivary glands. The only motivation they seem to have to accomplish anything is the utter hatred they feel toward the productive members of society who would so much as dare to suggest that they are not deserving of a governmental handout. The longer we deny and circumvent Darwinian principles and stay the process of natural selection (which coincidentally is the basic underlying principle of capitalism), the farther we drive ourselves down the road to ruin.

Charity should be the business of private persons, corporations and religious establishments, not the business of government. Government should only provide those few necessary services and leave the masses alone to direct their own destinies. The ultimate underlying theme is that horrible word "RESPONSIBILITY".

I am reminded of a group of individuals I had the misfortune of coming into contact with on a call where a woman requested an ambulance because she thought she was having a baby. The ambulance crew had been to the house before and had requested that police be dispatched with them due to some problems they had encountered the last time. The first thing that struck me as odd was the sign that was posted by the mailbox. It was a homemade wooden sign with sloppy handwriting on it that read, "WON'T WORK FOR FOOD."

I thought it was a joke until I made the trek down the long dirt driveway to the most rundown shack I have ever seen outside of a Burt Reynolds movie. This shack was in the middle of a garbage dump, or at least that's what the residents had made it look like. It had two or three rooms with no electricity, no running water and no place on the floor that wasn't covered with some sort of shit. I would swear that I felt things crawling on me the moment I walked inside.

There was a pile of clothes, or so it seemed, on the floor in a corner that served as the bed. That is where the woman was lying (and thankfully not laying). There were two men there also. All three of them stank to high heaven and so did everything in that place. It was all I could do to keep from vomiting when I walked in, though I think no one would have noticed if I had.

I was thankful to learn that the woman was not actually pregnant. In fact, through some sort of miracle she had had her tubes tied years before, according to the paramedics. Every other Friday or so the welfare check or some other government assistance check came in and they promptly traded it in for all the booze they could drink. Sometimes when she got really drunk the woman would start having some sort of delusion that she was having a baby.

Before we left I asked one of the men there about the sign that was by the mailbox.

"Damn right it's serious. I ain't got to work cuz the gubment sends us a check every week." (Not that it really matters, but for the record—these folks were Caucasian.)

I have spoken before of the people who 'blindly ignore the repeating lessons of history'. Our emerging welfare state is destined to be on the receiving end of the consequences of such actions. Those at the helm of the 'Good Ship Socialism' are steering our nation into a perilous and precarious position between the Scylla of over-taxation and the Charybdis of poverty-propagating entitlement programs. They are blindly ignoring the repeating lessons of countless countries where Socialism has failed miserably and the modest few where it has begrudgingly maintained a mediocre status quo. (Scylla and Charybdis are beasts from Greek mythology. Scylla had the face and torso of a woman, but from her flanks grew six dog heads. From her body there sprouted twelve canine legs and a fish's tail. The six heads would reach out and pluck sailors off of passing ships, devouring them. Charybdis was a monster who sucked in water forming a huge whirlpool and spewed it out in a large column three times a day. She lived in a cave at one side of the Strait of Messina or at Cape Skylla, opposite the monster Scylla, the two of them forming a dangerous threat to passing ships.)

Since the birth of our proud nation in 1776, the source of our unrivaled greatness has been Freedom—that most powerful of all human yearnings and the most essential of all human needs. Freedom was the irresistible magnet that drew the masses from varied cultures, nationalities and backgrounds all across God's green earth. People risked everything to come to America because they wanted nothing other than to guide their own destinies rather than having those destinies directed by some cold, mechanical government.

The trip to America was historically a difficult one. Consequently, people who would be likely to die in a garbage slide had neither the motivation nor the desire even to attempt such an endeavor. Our promise of Freedom drew only the strongest and the bravest and that is what made our country great. Now we must stand guard so that the vital characteristics of strength and courage are not bred from our proud bloodline.

Our blood is unique in that of all the nations in the world, it contains all the best qualities from all the races of the world. America became the greatest nation on Earth because our system was designed to allow anyone to reach his or her full potential, regardless of the height or depth of that potential. Unfettered by the shackles of tyranny and given nothing other than freedom, the people who chose to risk everything for a chance to be called "American" proved that given the opportunity, anyone can propel themselves to greatness or fade into obscurity based on their own actions and virtues.

Throughout the history of man, similar races have gathered within borders and isolated themselves into national units. Nations then jealously guarded their own unique cultures and called it Nationalism. Even to this day the word has benevolent connotations. When the great American "experiment" began, members from all those nations began to live and work together. Some held onto those 'noble' nationalist tendencies and set up communities here of similar cultures. The Irish lived in Irish neighborhoods, the Asian in Asian neighborhoods, the Russians in Russian neighborhoods. Etc. It is a practice that is still widespread today. It is another manifestation of basic human nature.

The problem arises when people cling to their old roots causing their natural tendency toward nationalism to be manifested on multiple, smaller scales. Then, conflicts that historically might have caused wars between entire nations result in disputes between communities or even smaller units of families or individuals. I would argue that the term 'racism' is one that owes its existence, in large part, to the American way of life. Since we are a nation of different peoples, rather than one people, what used to be called nationalism now has been renamed racism. To fix the problem, many people try to alter human nature. My experience in dealing with people as a law enforcement officer has shown me, time and time again, that human nature requires eons to evolve (and may never), not decades, years, or the stroke of a legislator's quill.

Prejudice and bias are immutable facets of human nature.

CONFRONTING EVIL

Anyone who tells you that he has no prejudice or bias is a liar. A much less negative sounding synonym for both of these words is preference. We all have individual preferences. They are not right or wrong, they just are. Whether we are rooting for our favorite sports team or trash talking people because they come from a rival school or city, we naturally gravitate towards groups that share our particular preferences. Birds of a feather, flock together.

I would argue that 'hate' is just a preference that has a strong negative emotion attached to it. None of these things are necessarily bad. What is bad is how you act based on your preferences. You and I both have an indisputable, God-given right to our particular preferences. We have the right to like or dislike anything or anyone for any reason. Hating someone is not a crime (yet), nor should it be.

Imagine a Jewish person who was a victim of Nazi atrocities. Is it unreasonable for someone with those life experiences to harbor resentment, prejudice, bias or hatred toward anything that reminded him or her of the Nazis? I would say that he has that right.

How about a young black man who spent the first twenty years of his life as the target for the hatred of a group of white people: would it be unreasonable for him to feel apprehension when in the company of white people, even if they were a different group entirely and one that had done nothing to warrant such feelings from him? After all, to him, white is white.

My grandmother was born in 1903. The Titanic sank when she was a little girl. She lived through the First World War, the Great Depression and was still in the prime of her life during World War II. She was one of the sweetest, kindest, and most loving people you would ever have the pleasure of meeting. She never had anything but kind words for anyone. She also refused to have anything in her house that was made in Japan. Hers was a sentiment left over from the bombing of Pearl Harbor and other atrocities perpetrated by the Japanese during the war. Whatever she felt about the Japanese, she kept to herself. She had a preference and that was her right.

Whether it's a style of music, clothing, food, cars, or whatever, people will always be prejudiced. To try to demean them because their prejudice is somehow not on the list of approved prejudices is just as prejudiced as any other prejudice. To try to change basic human nature to get rid of prejudice is foolish and impossible, so why waste energy trying?

What's my answer then? I suggest that we try to refocus that nationalist human nature on our relatively new nation. We need to realize that we are all Americans first and start pushing the concept of American nationalism. That's how we begin to overcome much of the infighting that pits race against race, culture against culture and group against group.

Of course there are many people who would be opposed to the elimination of racial strife in this country. Those are the people who make their living off of it. They are the race whores. I won't name any names but we all know who they are and they are everywhere. They capitalize on racial differences and do their very best to promote them and keep them alive. They add the strong negative emotion to people's natural preferences.

The concept is as old as time and has been exploited by some of history's greatest Evil. Adolph Hitler and Josef Stalin in the 1930s and 1940s, Slobodan Milosevic in the 1990s, and Osama Bin Laden in the 21st century are but a small sampling of the way that one man can exploit the preferences of a select group, convincing them that all their problems should be blamed on another select group. The leap to violence is not far behind.

CONFRONTING EVIL

I hope that in my lifetime I can see us at least begin to evolve away from that behavior and make the garbage start sliding the other way.

All that being said, I would like to take a moment to quote one of my own personal heroes and one of the great civil rights activists of the twentieth century. He is a conservative and staunch defender of our Constitution and of civil rights in general. He marched with Dr. Martin Luther King Jr. to Selma at a time when it wasn't popular to support civil rights; it was simply the right thing to do. He has spent the majority of his adult life fighting for the ideals espoused by the framers of our Constitution and the Bill of Rights. His words are as follows.

"I find it deplorable that we have insulated and isolated minority Americans from the ebb and flow of mainstream society and called it 'civil rights' and 'social welfare'. Socialism masquerading as civil rights has done little over the last thirty years except to disassociate and alienate one essential segment of our population.

The factors that eventually bring people together are often those that are measured on economic scales. Those made comfortable in a welfare system are those who eventually 'die' emotionally and psychologically in that same system. A 'father knows best' government mentality of providing all needs for all people has robbed an entire group of people of education, social skills, and simple good citizenship.

The cost has been high. Literally billions of dollars in tax money has been used to widen the gap of race and economic strata in America, rather than suture the wounds. Welfare programs have served primarily to *keep too many* people dependent upon government rather than to *free* people by giving them skills and an impetus to work and achieve something on their own.

We should all be skeptical about politicians who sermonize

about 'creating jobs'. The real goal should be to create 'employers'. Had government stepped aside to let a freer market provide better jobs and steady economic growth for all our citizens, racial and poverty issues would be much closer to resolution.

Dr. [Martin Luther] King opened the door to equality. The do-gooders who followed flaunted welfare as a shortcut to a better life. In fact, it was just slavery in another form, a modern incarnation of dependency on someone other than yourself.

Welfare thus turned out to be a crime cloaked in guilt. Its mindless, mechanized redistribution of wealth gave and gave and gave, while welfare recipients used and too many abused. The welfare culture forgot about one very important word that helps steer the ship of a free society: pride. Pride in ownership, pride in achievement, pride in accomplishment—such pride is directly related to freedom." (Quote from "The Courage To Be Free" by Charleton Heston pp 132-133 Saudale Press 2000.)

You will often hear the argument that a welfare system or entitlement program is actually a noble cause much like that of Robin Hood in England's dark ages. Let us not forget that, as the legend goes, Robin Hood was stealing from the rich aristocrats and government officials who had grossly abused their power, overtaxed and essentially robbed the citizenry of the hard earned fruits of their personal labors. He was not arbitrarily stealing from productive members of society just because they had more wealth than the average person. Therefore, an accurate application of the Robin Hood analogy would be if I, and other fine upstanding and hard working Americans like me, were to travel to any government outpost and forcibly extract a reasonable portion of our own tax dollars back from the government coffers. Please note that there is a huge difference in the two scenarios.

I am in no way saying, or even implying, that we should not

have compassion for the less fortunate or less blessed individuals in our society. On the contrary, there is no more moral or enlightened pursuit than providing a helping hand to your fellow man. What I am saying is that there are no long term social benefits to "spoon feeding" people all of their lives. The real benefit, both to the individual and to society as a whole, comes from helping people to become independent, self-sufficient, and responsible. We owe it to ourselves, our civilization, and to the future prosperity of all mankind, to teach people to fish, not give them one.

CHAPTER SEVENTEEN
You're in the Army Now...

In 2003, President Bush declared that a multinational coalition led by the United States would be going into Iraq for the purpose of enforcing sanctions that were imposed on that nation as a result of their defeat in the war that Saddam Hussein had initiated by his unprovoked invasion of his peaceful neighbor (Kuwait) in 1991. The terms of his surrender in the first Gulf War were all but ignored by this tyrant because he knew that President Clinton and the rest of the pacifist sissies on the planet (in conjunction with criminal nations like France, Germany and Russia who were working in concert with Saddam to exploit UN sanctions for monetary gain) would never do anything more to him than offer stern words of disdain. The way the world treated Saddam for twelve years was not at all unlike the way that the pansy-liberals in this country treat our criminals. The limit to the violence that these mental midgets (it's a metaphor, not an insult to dwarves or to little people) are capable of is the rhetorical equivalent of, "You better stop that right now...or I'll... tell you to stop it again!" Inevitably there is a quivering lower lip involved at some stage of this game.

I'll never forget an interview on TV just before the main assault on Iraq was to begin. A TV reporter had singled out an enlisted soldier to ask what that person thought of going into hostile territory. As if it were a perfectly natural response, the "soldier" (and I use the term loosely) said, "If I had known I was going to have to [fight], I never would have joined the Army."

Understand that every man or woman who decides to put on a police uniform is also joining an army and that the war is fought every day on every street and in every neighborhood across this great land. Our battle lines are undefined and our enemy can be around any or every corner. Our enlistment is measured in decades rather than years. We can go days, months or for some even years without seeing active combat yet we must be mentally prepared to face it every minute of every day. One thing that is for sure is that most of us will see active combat at some point in our careers. That is a very special and heavy burden—but Sheepdogs are a very special breed.

THE END

*There's nothing to read past here...especially if you are my Mom.

DO YOU SMOKE AFTER SEX?

The title of this chapter comes from an old joke. The punch line is, "I don't know—I never looked." Several of my friends had requested that I put some stories in this book that are just entertaining for their content and don't have any real points to make or lessons to learn. This entire chapter is dedicated to that mindless pursuit and contains some "mature subject matter." If you are offended by bad words, sex, blood, puss, ooze or any other cool, guy stuff, then stop reading now. For the rest of you here we go.

I'll start with an incident that happened when I was still in training and working on the morning watch. One of the three officers I had gone to the academy with pulled out on a suspicious person in a nearby public park. I heard an obvious amount of stress in his voice and started over to see what the source of that stress might be.

When he saw the lone vehicle parked in the closed county park, the officer, in conjunction with his FTO, decided to investigate. As he pulled up to the car and illuminated it with his patrol car's spotlight, it would be an understatement to say that he was taken aback by the sight of the particular drama that he beheld. The car did not have tinted windows so everything that was going on inside the nondescript, early seventies model sedan, was plainly visible.

There were two completely naked, reasonably attractive young women. One of the women was stretched out across the top of the bench seat, bracing herself by pressing one arm against the ceiling and the other against a rear door handle. She was deep in the throes of ecstasy as her legs were spread wide and between them was the other female. The second female was behaving as if she was having her last supper and her girlfriend was the long awaited dessert. The technical, legal definition of their activity was sodomy. "A person commits the offense of sodomy when he or she performs or submits to any sexual act involving the sex organs of one person and the mouth or anus of another." That law, thankfully, has since been repealed.

The two young women, unaffected by their sudden illumination, continued their course of action with a fervor one might accredit to the knights of the crusades. The officer, on the other hand, was so flustered by the XXX rated scene unfolding before him that as he exited his patrol car, he forgot to put the gearshift into "park". The resulting impact was minor but it was enough to stop the show and jar our lively young lasses from whatever realm they were in, back into ours. Aside from ample blushing on the part of all those involved (except the FTO of course), the situation was resolved without further incident and no paperwork was necessary.

The Urge

You would be surprised at how many people succumb to the "urge" while driving down the highway. While that, in and of itself, is not so unusual, there is a curious phenomenon whereby individuals who are feeling that urge, pull onto the shoulder of the roadway with their hazard lights on to satisfy that urge. I call it the "Pull onto the shoulder of the roadway with your hazard lights on to satisfy your urges" phenomenon.

One night in particular, I was working the evening watch and was the only unit that had a call to respond to. I was just clearing that call when our dispatcher advised us that the City of Atlanta Police were in a pursuit that was heading in our direction on the Interstate. At that time I heard a supervisor come over the radio with a phrase I never thought I would hear. That phrase was one that I have not heard since.

"Have all in service units respond to I-285 Eastbound at Roswell Rd to set up a rolling road block." You could practically hear the collective "Yeeehaw" that every officer on our shift had just let out. I stomped on the accelerator and put it in the wind. Despite my best efforts I was the last one to the roadblock and got there just in time to watch Evil circumvent the law enforcement corral by driving off of the Interstate via the creation of his own improvisational exit ramp through the grass and kudzu on the right shoulder of the roadway.

I was the last of the officers to join the pursuit that consisted of about twenty marked units from various jurisdictions, a half dozen or so unmarked detective cars and a helicopter that was operating the "Night Sun" spotlight that shone down relentlessly upon the car full of Evil.

We assumed the standard, single file formation that is so common in protracted car chases where the agencies have no alternative means by which they can halt the pursuit. Our only option in those days was to follow them until they either stopped of their own volition (like that will ever happen), ran out gas, crashed or crossed into Canada or Mexico.

This particular chase had been going on for over an hour and was reaching the point of monotony rather than the excitement that usually accompanies a good pursuit. Two other county units and I decided to push passed the pack of patrol cars up to the front. I was third in line when the front car gave a gentle nudge to the rear of Evil and as expected, Evil careened off the roadway into an empty parking lot.

By the time Evil's car came to a complete stop, it was surrounded on all sides by police cars. Throwing good tactics to the wind, we converged on the car like a swarm of locusts. Evil had locked the doors as if that would prevent us from taking further action and cause us all to get back into our cars and leave. Au contraire mon frere. I can honestly take credit for being the first one to enlist the aid of my 5-D-cell Maglite as an entry tool. One swift strike to the window and it exploded inward, showering Evil with nasty little shards of automotive safety glass. Within seconds, my fellow law enforcement officials chose to capitalize on my idea and all the side windows in Evil's car gave way in a similar manner. I distinctly remember seeing one officer on the trunk of the car furiously attacking the laminated rear windshield with the butt of his 12 gauge shotgun. Windshield glass is considerable tougher to break than side glass but that would not deter "Trunk Man".

It wasn't long before the front windshield was the only unbroken glass remaining and all the Evil had been forcefully extricated from what moments before had been a deadly missile rocketing through the streets of Atlanta. About then, a news truck seemed to appear from out of nowhere. Our supervisor was quick to order all the county units from the scene. We left as quickly and mysteriously as we had arrived.

It was on the trip back to the precinct that the sex enters the story. I had just gotten onto the highway when I noticed in the distance, an SUV pulled off to the right shoulder with its emergency flashers on. Being the dutiful public servant that I am, I pulled up behind the vehicle and activated my blue lights. I sat for a moment waiting for traffic to clear before approaching the car. I could tell there was someone inside and thought I noticed some movement. I cautiously approached the passenger window. The closer I got the more I could make out that the movement in the car was definitely a bouncing motion. As I moved even closer, I could see the image of a woman. She was straddling something in the passenger seat and was bouncing up and down on it much like the little kids do on the horsey rides at the amusement park or on their inflatable "hippity-hops".

As I got to a point literally right next to the woman, just outside of her window, her eyes opened. She looked me dead in the eye and smiled gently. Her motion, however, did not stop. If anything, it became more aggressive. I stood there stunned at her response to my presence and she said to me through the partially open window, "Give us just a second, I'm almost done." Thinking that was not an unreasonable request, I stepped a few steps back and let them finish. As soon as the bouncing stopped, I returned to the window to find the same woman. She was facing forward, but still smiling and looking me intently in the eye. For lack of anything better to say I said, "Next time don't put your flashers on."

"Yes sir," she said still smiling and off they drove.

That's Crazy

It's always a little difficult for a man, who for the most part was raised as a gentleman, to deal with naked women in a professional context. It is also difficult to get used to using violence against women when your entire life has been spent avoiding such. Put the two (nakedness and violence) together and the difficulty level is raised considerably. There's just so much conflict on so many different levels!

The man that called 911 that evening had found himself in an odd predicament. He had a whirlwind romance with someone whom he thought to be the woman of his dreams. They married after knowing each other for only a few weeks and within a few weeks of that unholy union, he started to get a glimpse of the real her. She was flat out crazy. Her personality shifts would give

Sybil a run for her money in the looney-lympics. I guess that's why Mom always told me to get to know a girl before you get too attached.

Anyway, she had nutted up in a bad way and began ranting something about Satan and sex and how all men were Evil and just wanted her body, etc., etc. He was getting scared and wanted us there to protect him while he packed his things to get the heck outta Dodge.

We conserved the peace until he got a chance to go and we left his wacky bride to her own devices. I didn't give much more thought to the encounter and went about my business. A hour or so later, I was patrolling the streets near where that call had been and I saw an old station wagon that was apparently broken down in the roadway. If I had been a little more observant, I would have remembered seeing that same car in the driveway of the crazy lady's house and I would have high-tailed it in the other direction. Unfortunately, it wasn't until the crazy lady got out of the car that I realized what I had stepped in. By then it was too late for a tactical withdrawal.(Retreat!)

She started on one of those crazy people rants that sane people could never accurately recount. She accused her now estranged husband of sabotaging her car as part of some sinister plot to force her to have sex with something. All four tires on her car were flat with no signs of damage. If I were a bettin' man I would say she parked the car in the road and let the air out via the valve stems.

Somehow I was able to talk her into driving the short distance back to her home and calling a cab to get wherever it was she felt the need to go. Foolish me left thinking that my time with the little demon was over.

Fast forward an hour or two to when a call came over the radio on a fight at one of the extended stay type hotels. I responded to the location not even considering the possibility that the same crazy woman was responsible for yet another call for police service. I spoke to the hotel manager who told me that a tenant in one of the rooms was yelling and screaming and it sounded like she was breaking things.

I went to the room in question and found the door standing open. Whoever was inside had definitely been breaking things. If I remember correctly, not one piece of furniture was intact. There was broken glass, turned over lamps, broken and upside down furniture and holes in the walls that looked fresh. The room was lighted by a single lamp that was lying horizontally on the floor with only the bare burning bulb remaining. There was some secondary light coming from the bathroom that added little to the eerie scene. The room was strangely quiet at that point and I was almost convinced that the perpetrator had left.

Just as I crossed the plane of the doorway into the room, leaving my backup standing guard in the hallway, a naked female emerged from the bathroom. She took one look at me and let out a blood curdling scream. Then she started picking up various objects of broken hotel property which she promptly hurled in my direction. I will confess that I suffered from an internal conflict because, quite frankly, despite the ongoing assault, without her clothes on she was a hottie. She was still yelling some of those things that crazy people yell when I jumped over the overturned sofa and tackled her naked ass in a very professional and nonsexual manner. It took surprisingly little effort to get her under control. I dragged her out to the parking lot and threw her into the patrol car. I directed the backup unit to look for some clothes for her while I contacted a supervisor to make sure he knew about this potentially compromising situation.

After several minutes, my backup unit emerged with the news that there were no clothes anywhere in the hotel room. She was going to have to go to jail in her birthday suit. No big deal. She wasn't the first and certainly would not be the last, even if she was the best looking. I requested that a unit accompany me to the jail to help prevent any potential false accusations of impropriety.

As we started on the twenty to thirty minute ride to the jail, the crazy lady was uncharacteristically quiet. That silence was soon broken when I noticed her butt pressed firmly against the plexiglass screen that separated us. I had a perfect view of her butt and her genital area through the screen, though they were markedly deformed by the pressure she applied against them. Somehow she managed to work her handcuffed hands over her arched waist. She then managed to start masturbating with her butt in the air. While she violently "pleasured" herself she started screaming, "Why don't you just stop this car and fuck me now you bastards. You know you want to stick your dicks in me. You're all the same. Pull the fucking car over and fuck me now. I can take you both…"

Mixed with some more of the crazy people talk, she implored us to attempt to satiate her sexually throughout the ride to the jail. Apparently, we were not special. As we left the jail I could hear her screaming something quite similar to the throng of deputies that had gathered to usher her into her new temporary quarters.

For those of you noting an inconsistency between this incident and the one with the crazy computer kid, the reason this woman went to jail was because this incident occurred early in my career when the jail had the facilities for dealing with crazy people. Now those facilities are exclusive to our public hospital.

CONFRONTING EVIL

Pettus Eatus Facius

Ask any pet owner if their particular pet is unique and they will invariably begin to describe their pet's "personality". After years of careful deliberation, I have come to the quite unpopular conclusion that animals are more like living machines and that any semblance of a personality is really just an effort on the owner's part to impart some special significance on their particular animal and to justify in their own minds all the love and attention that they devote to those animals. There's no doubt a link to all the children's stories and cartoons that depict animals as thinking and feeling creatures with human characteristics that contribute to this unique form of what could feasibly be called a psychopathology.

I know I am probably going to make some enemies with that proposition but hey, it's just one guy's opinion. I happen to be a pet owner/animal lover and really don't see anything wrong with it: I just don't think that my animals are some intelligent, sentient beings trapped in a beastly form. They are just animals. Similar animals have similar "personalities" which I tend to think are just instinctive, preprogrammed behaviors that we attach way too much significance to.

Regardless of whether you agree or not I would like to explore one unique behavior that seems to be common to many different species of house pet. The first time I saw this peculiar behavior was when I was called to check on the welfare of an elderly woman that lived alone with her two cats. Her family lived out of state and had been unable to contact her and requested that we try to make contact.

To make a long story short, it turned out that the old lady had died of natural causes several days before we were called to check on her. When we first found her, all the skin on her face was gone. What was left was exposed muscle tissue that was in a surprisingly well-preserved state. The muscles were a dark red color and looked a lot like the pictures you see in anatomy books. Since the lips were gone, the teeth were completely exposed making the corpse appear to be grinning at some undisclosed hilarity.

The eyeballs were still intact but the eyelids were missing. Consequently, the eyeballs appeared to protrude un-naturally from their sockets and had a very eerie stare that you would swear followed you around the room. To be quite frank, the ladies head looked fake—like something you would see at a Halloween haunted house or something.

What happened to her is something that happens fairly frequently when a corpse is left in a house with some hungry house pets. The animals ate all the skin off of her face. I am sure that there is some scientific name for this particular behavior but since I don't know what it is I'll just make one up. Let's call it *pettus eatus facius*. I have heard speculation that the animals only eat the face away because they don't want to be reminded of their dead master or some other such nonsense. I would be willing to bet that there is a much less interesting explanation like "The stupid animal was hungry and the best tasting thing it could find was the exposed skin of the dead person's face." Call me crazy but that whole Occam's razor thing that says the simplest explanation is probably the correct one seems to grab me here.

Maybe someone can do a doctoral thesis on the subject and find some psychic animal mind reader or reincarnation specialist to really delve into the heart of this truly mysterious phenomenon and answer that burning question once and for all. Until that day comes, I guess whenever we come across a similar scene we will just have to wonder as we stare and say, "Hey. That's pretty damn disgusting."

CONFRONTING EVIL

You Picked A Fine Time To Leave Me Loose Wheel

I was parked on an entrance ramp one night pretending to watch for speeders while desperately trying to keep my eyes open when I was startled to life by a loud bang that was fairly close. I looked across the highway just in time to see a car smash headlong into the facing end of a temporary concrete retaining wall. This was one of those walls that the construction crews make out of the concrete k-rails to keep traffic from crashing into the construction sites.

The car hit the wall with such force that the back end of the car came up off of the ground several feet before it came crashing back to Earth. I immediately notified my dispatcher and requested an ambulance as I headed for the accident scene. All I had to do was go the wrong way down the opposing exit ramp and I was at the scene in no time at all. When I got there, the driver of the car was out of the vehicle. He was obviously stunned and disoriented and as I got closer I discovered why.

He had been driving down the roadway, minding his own business, when all of a sudden, his right rear axle just snapped, which was apparently the sound that had awakened me. The right rear of the car slammed to the pavement as the wheel rolled on past the car, continuing in its original direction of travel. The added friction from the scraping of the right rear of the car on the ground caused it to jerk to the right just as the car approached the concrete wall. The poor guy really didn't have much of a chance to steer the car away and the result was the crash that I had witnessed.

The driver had elected not to wear his seatbelt that night and as a result of that less than prudent decision, upon striking the concrete wall, he flew headlong into the windshield. His head pierced the glass and actually went about halfway out of the vehicle before the inertia of the sudden stop slammed him back to the rear. The laminated glass caught on his cheeks as his direction reversed and the glass literally ripped off most of the guys face, leaving it stuck behind in the shattered remnants of the windshield.

The arterial bleeding was so bad that he was spewing visible streams of steamy hot blood several feet out from where he stood. I couldn't get close to him without being sprayed so I tried to yell to him to use his shirt as a compress to cap the gusher. He had enough presence of mind to follow my direction and though he had to have extensive reconstructive surgery, he was lucky enough to survive the ordeal. Let it suffice to say he would probably never need to waste his money on a Halloween mask ever again.

ABOUT THE AUTHOR

Richard Nable was born and raised in the state of Georgia. He graduated from the University of Richmond, VA in 1987 with a bachelor's degree in biology and promptly went to work as a police officer for a major metropolitan police department in the Southeastern United States. After crushing crime on the front lines for over seventeen years, in 2005 FTO/Sgt. Nable was transferred to a full time position as second in command at his department's firing range. As a certified firearms instructor and general weapons enthusiast he is SWAT and counter-sniper certified. In addition to firearms, he continues to train both rookie and veteran officers in a variety of police related curricula such as law, search and seizure, use of force, officer survival and tactics, vehicle pullovers, courtroom testimony and numerous other topics. He is also a nationally certified driving instructor and teaches basic defensive driving as well as high speed and pursuit driving. He is an active member of the Georgia Association of Law Enforcement Firearms Instructors, The Association of Professional Law Enforcement Emergency Vehicle Response Trainers International and a lifetime member of the National Rifle Association. His first book, "Searching For Evil…and the Perfect Donut" received wide acclaim both in the law enforcement and civilian worlds alike. While this book is not a sequel in the traditional sense, it does carry on some of the tones set in the first book while adding some new topics, themes and styles that are guaranteed to entertain and educate.